I0170800

★Pack Up & Leave★

To my sweet children:
Our adventures
wouldn't be the same without you…
I'm glad that when it's time to
PACK UP & LEAVE
you're so ready and willing
to tag along

Pack Up & Leave

Travel Tips for
Fun Family Vacations

By Jennifer Flanders

Prescott Publishing
Tyler, Texas

Copyright © 2019, Jennifer Flanders

Cover design, interior design, and typesetting:
Jennifer Flanders

Cover photos:
https://www.nicepng.com/ourpic/u2q8r5t4y3r5q8u2_suitcase-clipart-packed-suitcase-relocated-we-have-moved/ (front)
David Flanders Photography (back)

Publisher:
Prescott Publishing
3668 Southwood Drive
Tyler, TX 75707
http://prescottpublishing.org

Pack Up & Leave: Fun Ideas for Traveling with Children
ISBN: 978-1-938945-37-3
Library of Congress Control Number:2019943221

Unless otherwise noted, all Scripture references are taken from THE NEW AMERICAN STANDARD BIBLE ®, Copyright ©1960, 1962, 1963, 1968, 1971, 1972, 1973, 1975, 1977, 1995 by the Lockman Foundation. Used by permission.

The ideas and suggestions espoused in this book are not intended as a substitute for consulting with a physician. This book is intended as a reference volume only, not as a medical manual. Neither the author nor the publisher shall be liable or responsible for any loss or damage allegedly arising from any information or suggestion in this book. Mention of specific companies, organizations, or authorities in this book does not imply endorsement by the authors or publisher, nor does mention of specific companies, organizations, or authorities imply that they endorse this book, its authors, or the publisher.

- CONTENTS -

Section 4: Packing Pointers

Section 5: On the Road Again

Section 6: Happy Diversions

Section 7: A Lifestyle of Learning

Section 8: Grab Some Grub on the Go

Section 9: Extra Savings

Section 10: Home Away from Home

Section 11: Savvy Souvenirs

Section 12: Expect the Unexpected

Section 13: Traveling with Baby

Section 14: International Travel

- FOREWORD -

For as long as I can remember, I've wanted to travel the world. But when I got married early (at age 20), and we started having kids right away, I assumed I'd have to wait until retirement to pursue that dream.

Rather than put it off, however, my wife and I eventually decided to go early and take the children with us. And I'm so glad we did.

As a result, our kids have developed a love for travel, too. They've been to so many exciting and interesting places, not only with family, but also on their own: Language school in Costa Rica. Dog sledding in Arctic circle. Student exchange program in Japan. Summer school at Cambridge in England. Babysitting in Qatar. Military service in Germany. Working with orphans in Nepal. Medical mission trips to Honduras and Guatemala. The list goes on.

But as with so many of life's blessings, travel experiences are better when shared. And when you can share them with your family, it makes them even more meaningful.

This is partly because we reference such shared experiences often: *Remember when the streets flooded in Venice? Can you believe it snowed on us in Paris? Weren't those gyros we ate in Munich delicious? That reminds me of the falcon we held in Budapest. Wasn't it funny when that camel spit at Dad?*

Yes, our travels provide us with wonderful memories, interesting stories, and important reference points. Whether traveling with parents or on their own, our kids have gained not only an appreciation of other cultures, but an even greater appreciation for their own.

So if you've been putting off your travel dreams until your kids are older or you're ready to retire, rethink your plans. This book contains a wealth of ideas for making family travel more fun, enjoyable, educational, and *easy*.

So make the necessary arrangements to *pack up and leave* as soon as possible, taking your children along for the ride. In the end, you'll be glad you did.

Have fun, and God bless!
- Doug Flanders, MD

- INTRODUCTION -

My husband first suggested we take a coast-to-coast road trip back when we had only seven children. At that time, the baby was still breastfeeding, and her six older siblings seldom sat still.

Although I loved my family dearly—*and still do*—the thought of packing sufficient and sundry supplies for so many little ones then spending several hours a day, for weeks on end, strapped into an overstuffed Suburban seemed like more trouble than it could possibly be worth.

Boy, was I ever wrong!

Not about it requiring a lot of work. *It did.* But about how entirely gratifying and educational and enjoyable traveling with kids can be.

What began as a halfhearted attempt to humor my husband's harebrained idea quickly became a pastime we pursue with a passion.

For us, family travel is a way of life. It's an opportunity to see the world, to experience other cultures, to meet new and interesting people, to see strange and exotic sights. It gives us time to bond with one another and make many marvelous memories with our children.

We cherish all these things.

We've made mistakes, certainly. Like when we accidentally left a child at the Air Force Academy and made it across town before realizing he wasn't with us. Our next stop, ironically, was *Focus on the Family*—exactly what we'd failed to do.

Or when I prepaid for a rental car to drive on our Florida honeymoon, only to learn when we arrived that neither my husband nor I were allowed to drive it. He was too young, and I didn't have a valid license. (*Why renew on my birthday when I'd have to change it again a few months later once I was married?*) Technically, that trip was taken before kids, but we learned an important lesson, nonetheless.

Similar goof-ups taught us the importance of checking (and re-checking) hours of operation. And time zone changes. And admission policies. And age restrictions.

Or finding out if a restaurant accepts credit cards or only deals in cash (preferably *before* we order and eat our food!).

Or whether the hotel address we pull up on Google maps matches the one on our actual reservation—thus preventing the need to drive 30 miles out of the way late at night to reach it, when we could've been in bed a long time ago had we stopped at the right hotel, the one we passed on the way.

With all that potential for disappointment, is it any wonder I became such a stickler for making detailed itineraries?

Even so, we've learned a few tips and tricks along the way that make traveling with kids—even a dozen of them—less work and more fun.

I've happily shared my methods with other parents over the years, albeit in a piecemeal fashion. I've written some blog posts on the subject. Answered friends' questions. Given a few talks. I even did an hour-long workshop on the topic at a couple of big homeschool conventions last year.

As I watched convention-goers furiously scribbling notes and screenshotting slides during my presentations, it dawned on me that lots of families are hungry for help in this area.

They'd like to travel with their kids, but are overwhelmed by the work involved. Some want tips for making vacations more affordable. Some are looking for help with the planning. Some want detailed packing lists. Others need fresh ideas for their next destination.

Which is precisely why I wrote this book. In it, you'll find all those answers and more. I hope these ideas will help your family set a course for adventure.

Go together. Have fun. Save money. And while you're at it, make lots of delightful memories that will last a lifetime!

Safe travels,

Jennifer Flanders

Section 1

Motivation & Mindset

-1-

Collect Moments Not Things

I spotted this admonition on an airport mural last time our family traveled overseas: "Collect moments, not things."

It was a good reminder. We were backpacking Europe at the time, and every souvenir and memento we carried home would make our packs just a little heavier. That meant extra weight we didn't need on our shoulders—or in our lives.

How much better to focus on the time at hand. To be present *in the moment*. To savor the memories we were making with our children, rather than scouring our surroundings for some trinket to commemorate our travels… or even another group photo to prove we were there! With a crew as large as ours, I've had to learn to be very selective about posed photo ops. Otherwise, I'll wear everyone out with my incessant pleas to "smile for the camera."

The wonderful thing about collecting memories instead of stuff is that you don't need to travel to the other side of the globe to get started. Being fully *present* is something you can do right where you are, right now—even if it's just within the four walls of your own home. Start there, then marvel at how far that mindset will take you.

3

-2-
Broaden Your Horizons

One of the reasons we love to travel with our children is because it gives them the opportunity to see beyond their own small corner of the world. It broadens their horizons and enriches their education by exposing them to a wide variety of people, places, and experiences.

But travel in and of itself is not enough to accomplish such goals. No matter how new or exotic a child's surroundings, the benefits will be lost if his eyes are glued to a screen and his ears tuned into a headset. (That goes for adults, too.)

Good news is, you can begin broadening children's horizons right where you are by teaching them to look at the world around them with fresh eyes. Train them to notice things in their peripheral vision that might otherwise have escaped their attention.

Get to know the people who cross your path and ask them a lot of questions. Find out about their origins and upbringing. Consider their perspective on life and note how it differs from your own.

If you'll make this way of thinking a habit, then when you do get an opportunity to travel, you'll be on track to make the most of the experience.

4

-3-

Bond as a Family

One of the nicest benefits of traveling with children is the opportunity it provides for family bonding. There's something about being away from all your day-to-day responsibilities allows you to connect in a way that rarely happens otherwise.

There are a couple of things parents can do to maximize this opportunity: First, as much as possible, *participate* in all the outings and activities. Instead of reading a book at water's edge, jump in the pool *with* your kids. Play Marco Polo or Sharks & Minnows.

Build sandcastles together at the beach. Sit side by side on amusement park rides. Hike together along nature trails. The more active (and joyful) your involvement in the things your child loves, the stronger the bond you'll build as a result.

Second, take advantage of increased time together to *communicate* with your kids. Share your favorite childhood memories, tell them what you think about the world around you. Discuss goals and beliefs and aspirations.

Just as importantly, ask your children about their thoughts and impressions, hopes and dreams, and listen attentively to how they answer.

-4-
Experience Different Cultures

Although traveling to another country is an excellent way to experience other cultures, it isn't the only way (nor the most economical). To introduce your children to other cultures, try a few of the following ideas—no passport required:

- read a book about the country that interests you
- Google pictures or coloring pages of the country
- watch a documentary about the people who live there
- study the history, art, and music of the country
- find it on a map and learn about its topography
- research different routes for getting there
- eat at a restaurant that serves the country's cuisine
- learn to prepare one of its popular dishes yourself
- study the language spoken in that country
- dress in the traditional garb of its citizens
- get to know an international student from the area

If you're already booked passage for an international trip? These activities are for you, too. Not only will they help you prepare for the journey, but doing them before you go will greatly enrich the time you spend abroad.

-5-
Learn & Grow

Curiosity and enthusiasm are contagious. I know of no better way to cultivate in your children an intense love for learning than to model the same yourself. If you're excited about where you're going and what you're learning, you children are sure to pick up on that fact.

Knowledge should be a lifelong pursuit for all of us. When it comes to traveling, that is part of the draw: the thrill of exploration and discovery and adventure. Going new places. Meeting new people. Trying new things.

Encourage your children to ask questions. Asking questions will develop their minds and help them grow. Which will inevitably lead to more and better and deeper questions.

If you find yourself growing weary of your child's endless queries and insatiable curiosity, don't attempt to stifle it, but rather seek a way to channel it.

Check out books at the library on topics that interest them. Direct them to documentaries that answer their questions. Arrange for factory tours in the fields that intrigue them, conducted by insiders who can provide behind-the-scene glimpses into the way things work (more on this in Chapter 52).

-6-
See Things through Your Children's Eyes

Remember what it was like to be a child yourself. That wasn't so long ago that you can't recall it, right?

Seeing the world through the eyes of your children means sharing their wonder and enthusiasm for the things you're experiencing. Laugh and play together. Let your love for each other and your zest for life bond you together.

Of course, on the flip side of the coin, viewing the world as a child means being sensitive to your little ones' limitations. Remember how cramped the back car seat felt when you were the one riding in it? Or how endless the hours on long road trips? Like you might *never* arrive at your destination?

Keep those things in mind during your planning, as well. Schedule plenty of stretch breaks and rest stops when traveling cross country. Alternate visits to stuffy, adult-oriented museums with child-friendly discovery centers.

If you're visiting relatives who think children should be seen and not heard, break up hours of monotonous sitting-still-on-the-couch-and-listening-to-boring-conversation with a walk around the block or a trip to the neighborhood park. That'll make more pleasant memories for everyone.

Section 2

Come Up with a Plan

-7-

Define Your Goals

Before starting to plan, give some thought to what you hope to accomplish with your travels. Will this be...

- a family vacation? Are you looking for time to bond with your children and to create lasting memories together?

- a business trip? If you must travel for work, can you take family along, too? They can go sightseeing while you're on the job, then meet up with you once you're done for the day.

- a romantic getaway? Do you need an opportunity to reconnect as a couple? Maybe an anniversary trip or second honeymoon?

- an away game? If you're kids play on sport teams and have to travel for out-of-town games, perhaps you can make a long weekend of it and explore the town once the game is over.

You get the idea. The purpose of your trip will largely determine the backbone of your itinerary. So it's always best to begin there.

-8-
Set a Budget

The first step in planning a trip is determining how much you have to spend.

We know from experience that great vacations don't have to cost a fortune. And there are plenty of smart ways to save, even on the essentials (see Sections 8-9).

Nevertheless, you'll need to consider the associated costs as you plan your trip. At a minimum, these should include the following categories.

GAS MONEY: How far away is your destination? What kind of gas mileage does your car typically average? What is the current price of gas at home? On the road?

ACCOMODATIONS: Where will you stay? What will it cost? Are there less expensive options where you're headed?

FOOD: What will you eat while you're gone? Will you have access to a kitchen where you can cook your own meals, or will you eat out most of the time. Does your hotel include free breakfast? Are there staples you can bring from home?

ENTERTAINMENT: What will you do when you get there? Does it cost money? Are there any discounts available?

-9-
Start Small

If your children are young, or if you've not done much traveling together in the past, don't get too ambitious right out of the starting gate.

Get your toes wet before diving into the deep end. Rather than planning a 5000-mile cross-country road trip or a month long backpacking excursion across Europe, start small.

Try a long weekend a bit closer to home – preferably no more than three or four hours away. Check into a hotel and see a few sights or pitch a tent and take a short hike.

Whatever it is you'd like to do on your big dream trip, see if you can get a small taste of something similar on your overnight trip.

That way, you can get a better feel for what your kids can handle at their current age. You can troubleshoot while stakes are small and adjust plans accordingly.

And as a bonus, you'll still create some great memories with these starter trips. At this writing, my own children have traveled all over the world, but they still rank as some of their very fondest memories those long weekends we spent in the next state over, just a few hours from home.

-10-
Consider Age & Ability

Do your best to recall what it was like to be your child's age. What do you remember? What do you wish you could forget?

My family didn't do a lot of traveling when I was growing up, but when we did, it felt like such a wonderful adventure! Everything was exciting to me.

The things I especially liked were outdoor activities like strolling through botanical gardens, visiting amusement parks, or zipping down water slides. I also fondly remember visiting museums, libraries, and historical homes. That was before the era of hands-on exhibits, so my parents were smart to keep those stops short—just as my husband and I tried to do when our own children were little.

The things I didn't like? Riding in the car for long stretches of time and hunting for hotels in crowded tourist towns with few vacancies.

Back when I was growing up, three hours cooped up in a car seemed like an eternity. *And that was before seatbelts!* So now, whenever our family hits the road for an extended trip, I allot plenty of time for smelling roses along the way—and book our hotels well in advance (the Internet makes it easy).

-11-
Compile a Bucket List

If you enjoy traveling, you may want to draw up a list of all the sights you hope to someday see. Group them in whatever way that makes sense to you: by state or geographical region or in order of importance.

That way, you can tick them off as you go, perhaps even fitting several in on one trip. Heading cross-country to California? Consider stopping by the Grand Canyon on your way.

Sure, the Grand Canyon is magnificent enough to warrant a trip of its own, but you only have about 18 years before your kids start leaving home, so why not double up when you can? Spending three hours at the South Rim while you're in the general area sure beats never seeing it at all.

Our family hasn't taken a dedicated trip to Washington, DC, but we've traveled through a couple of times on our way to New York. Would you believe we packed most of the Presidential Memorials, several Smithsonian Museums, and a tour of the Capitol Building into just 24 hours? We did!

But the reason any of those outings were even on our radar is because they were first on our bucket list. What's on yours?

-12-
Break Out the Maps

One of our sons has a real passion for maps. Even as a toddler, he would pore over our family's atlas every night as his father read story time. By now, he has most major world cities memorized and can recognize them instantly by skylines or road configurations.

I'm nowhere near as knowledgeable as he is when it comes to having an internal GPS, but I do love to zoom out and consider the the big picture whenever I'm planning a trip.

That's where my bucket list comes in handy. As I plan the route we'll take to a given destination, I try to take into consideration the path's proximity to other things we'd like to fit in along the way.

Whenever possible, we take a different route home from the one we took to get there, so as to mark even more bucket list items off on the trip back.

But what if your travels take you nowhere near a bucket list item? Well, I've got some great tips for adding interest to those journeys, too, which we'll discuss at length in Section 7. In the meantime, why not ask your travel companions to share their ideas and opinions?

-13-
Poll the Kids

During the eight years my husband spent in med school and residency, he seldom got more than three days off in a row. Our family's go-to vacation spot during that hectic era was Hot Springs, Arkansas—primarily because we could drive there from Dallas in four hours. We spent many a Memorial Day there, window shopping on Central Avenue, touring Bathhouse Row, hiking around the park, visiting the springs, feeding alligators, and swimming in Lake Hamilton.

Once Doug graduated, 15 years passed without our visiting Arkansas at all. Then our kids requested we go back for old time's sake. Before the return trip, I made a list of every activity we'd previously done in Hot Springs (plus a few we hadn't) and had everyone rate them on a scale from 0 to 3:

> 0 = I'd rather skip this altogether
> 1 = I'm willing to participate if everyone else does
> 2 = It sounds fun, but isn't my top priority
> 3 = I'll be disappointed if we *don't* do this

Rather than just guessing what everyone would enjoy, use a poll to make sure you're doing the things that matter most to those traveling with you. And if one activity generates both zeroes *and* threes? Split up! Let the girls browse the antique stores while the boys go jet skiing. Or *vice versa.* ☺

17

-14-
Draw Up an Itinerary

O nce I know where we're going and how we'll get there, I create a day-by-day itinerary, beginning with a list of all the days we'll be gone. To this I add:

- Starting and ending points for each day on the road
- The color shirt we'll wear each day: this streamlines packing, makes headcounts faster, and ensures beautifully coordinated souvenir snapshots to glue in our scrapbooks! (see Chapter 27)
- Reservation information: hotel name, address, phone number, rate, and confirmation number
- Reminders to set our clocks forward or back as we cross into different time zones
- Any planned stops: hours of operation, entry fees, and special notes (e.g. "free admission on Tuesday")
- Notes about audiobooks for the road (e.g., if we'll listen to Thomas Jefferson's biography on the way to Monticello, I put it on my packing list and also add a reminder to that day's schedule)
- A list of chores to do before leaving town: hold mail, empty trash, turn off lights, lock doors, etc.
- An itemized packing list, including any out-of-the-ordinary items such as life-jackets (if we're going to the coast), heavy coats (if we're headed to the mountains), or antibiotics for a child who has an ear infection

-15-
Something for Everyone

We traveled through Oregon several years ago and were amazed at how clear the rivers and green the foliage and fresh the air and bright the flowers were at every turn. What a gorgeous state!

But when my father-in-law followed the same route a few months later, he wasn't impressed: *"Too much vegetation!"* he told us matter-of-factly. Doug's dad prefers desert sands to dense woodlands.

The point is, everybody is different. What thrills one person may bore another.

So take this fact into consideration and vary your vacation plans—both from one day to the next in terms of activities, but also from one year to the net in terms of destinations.

Remember: variety is the spice of life! Go to the beach one year, the mountains the next, the desert the next. Alternate indoor and outdoor activities. Break up energy-draining outings with restful days spent relaxing by the pool or playing board games in the cabin.

This will allow you to accommodate differing tastes and personalities—and expand everybody's scope of experience.

Section 3

Shoestring Vacations

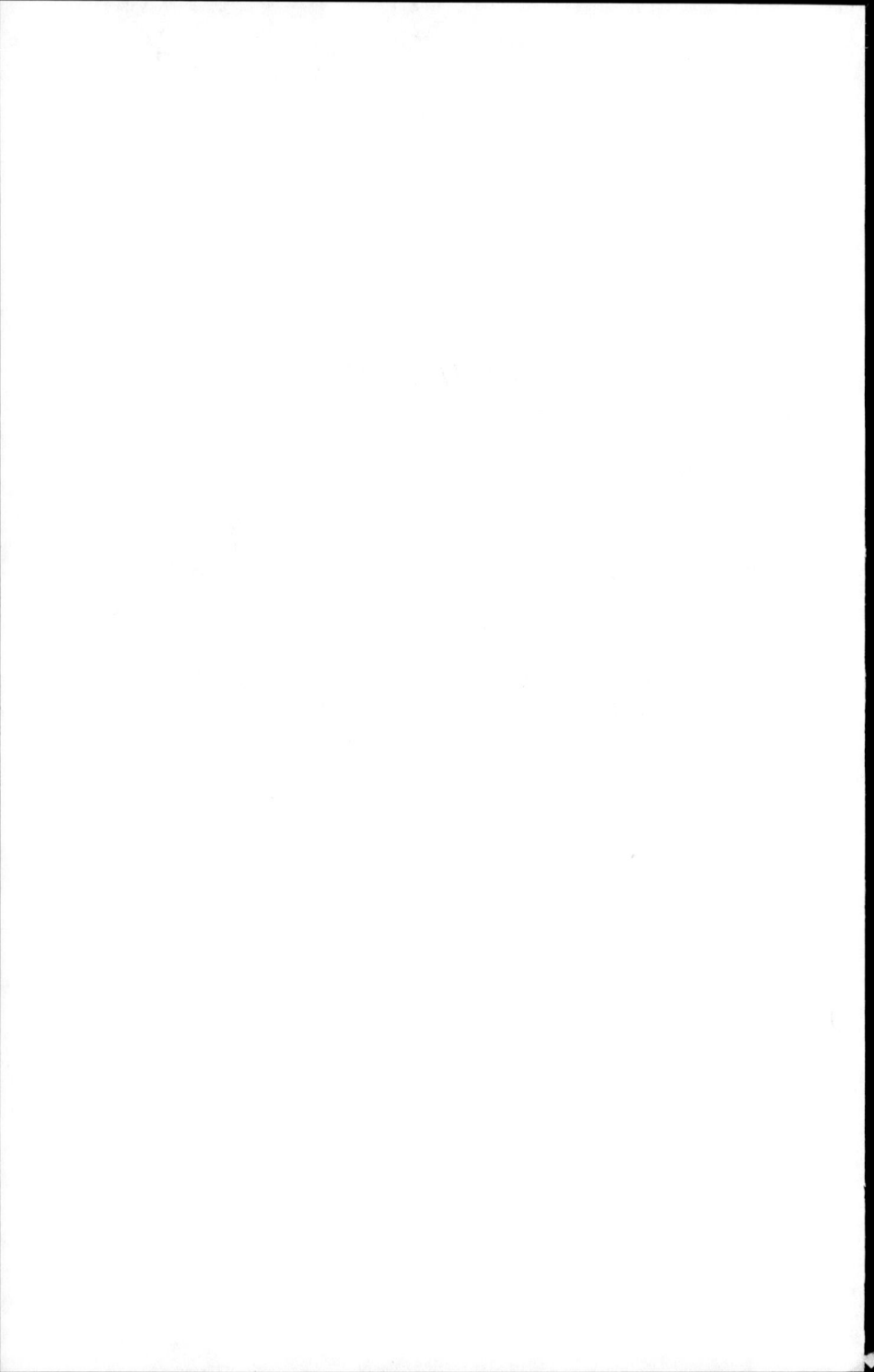

-16-
Plan a Staycation

You don't have to travel far from home to enjoy a wonderful vacation with your family. You can save both time and money by playing the part of a tourist right in your own hometown:

- Take in local museums, zoos, parks, and gardens
- Search out historical homes, markers, and other points of interest
- Check with your Chamber of Commerce to see if any festivals, concerts or movies-in-the-park are planned during your days off
- Play Putt-Putt golf or go bowling as a family
- Host a family reunion—let the family come to you!

If your budget allows it, you might even check into a nearby hotel for a night of two. Go swimming in their pool and enjoy a free breakfast buffet the next morning.

I'm sure you can think of other fun things to do close to home. Keep a list of all your options for future reference. Your first staycation may be so successful that you'll want to plan another.

Plus, your list will be a great resource to share with any out-of-town guests who visit you throughout the year.

-17-
Enjoy a Long Weekend

If you can't find enough to do in your own back yard, try traveling just a few towns over.

A distance of one to four hours away from home makes for a nice getaway over a long weekend.

If you live in the city, you may want to look for a quaint, quiet little town where you can relax and enjoy a slower pace for a few days.

If you're accustomed to rural life, you might prefer to head to the city and enjoy a wider variety of things to do. Big cities always have a lot going on—including much you can do for free (refer Section 7).

Get out a map and draw a circle with a one- to two-hundred-mile radius with your town at the center. Investigate every dot inside that border. Do you spot any places that pique your interest? Some city you've wanted to visit in the past but never found time to do so?

If so, Google the town's name. Find out what they have to offer in terms of sightseeing, museums, or other attractions. Then make a reservation at a local hotel and go for it!

-18-
Bigger Isn't Better

It's always a good idea to consider the ROI (Return On Investment) when making vacation plans. "More lavish and expensive" does not always translate into "better family bonding or more cherished memories."

In fact, spending more often just leads to higher stress, worse headaches, and more unrealistic expectations—not to mention smaller bank accounts! You have to work harder to afford the vacation before you take it, and wait longer to recover (both physically and financially) once it's over.

So don't feel pressured to keep up with the Joneses. Even if everyone else you know is spending a bundle to stand in long lines on a hot day wearing mouse ears at an amusement park, that doesn't mean you have to join the crowd.

Our kids were nearly grown before we finally made *that* trip, and none of them feel like they missed out. We had a blast taking far less expensive vacations for the bulk of their childhoods and saved the Magical Kingdom until we could better afford it. By that time, they were old enough to remember the trip, smart enough to resist overpriced souvenirs, fast enough to sprint to the rides with the shortest lines, and mature enough to have a fun time without anyone throwing a temper tantrum because he missed his nap.

-19-
Think Outside the Box

Vacations come in all shapes and sizes. Don't get stuck thinking yours has to look a certain way. You don't have to model your time off on what family or friends are doing with theirs. Or even on what you've done in the past. Be willing to think outside the box.

One viable option you may not have considered is bartering. If you live in the mountains and your friend lives at the beach, investigate the possibility of swapping homes for a week. That would provide each family a place to stay, as well as a good resource for interesting things to do in the area while you're there.

If you can't barter houses, how about bartering skills? Would any of your family or friends be willing to host your crew in exchange for help with a building project or some other kind of skilled work in your area of expertise.

We've stayed in host homes while doing mission work and speaking at homeschool conventions. We have a friend who teaches water aerobics classes in exchange for summer lodging at a swanky resort, and another friend who teaches literature classes aboard a cruise ship for the Semester at Sea program. Set your mind to it. No telling what non-traditional vacation options you'll come up with!

26

-20-
Travel Documentaries

Sometimes, even the best laid plans go awry. I can think of at least three instances in the past thirty years when circumstances forced us to abandon our vacation plans.

Most recently, our family was scheduled to spend a week in Wisconsin Dells. We were to leave on our daughter's eighth birthday. I'd made reservations, mapped out the route, had our bags packed and ready to go. Then, three hours before time to pull out of the driveway, our birthday girl got violently ill. We tried to just delay the trip a day or two, but by our daughter recovered, one of her brothers had succumbed. Then another. Then another.

Whenever this happens, we simply change gears. We cancel our reservations, adjust our expectations, and try to make the best of our unexpected days at home.

We've learned that even when our bodies can't travel, we can travel in our minds. So we grab our quilts and throw-up buckets and all our individual Gatorade bottles and gather together to watch some cool documentaries on faraway lands we've never been to before. Travel films make a pretty good substitute when you can't make the journey yourself. One day, after the present illness has passed, maybe we'll visit some of those places in person.

27

-21-
Backyard Camping

Although adults seem pretty polarized over the prospect of tent camping, I've yet to meet a little kid who doesn't thrill at the thought of sleeping out under the stars.

When it comes to "roughing it," you have lots of options. You can camp out at state parks, in national forests or grasslands, and even on some beaches. Try googling "where can I camp for free?" to find a good place to pitch a tent near you.

If your children are very young, however, I would suggest first giving it a trial run in your own backyard. That's what we did as soon as we bought our first tent, and our kids loved it!

We dragged our pillows and sleeping bags outside, zipped ourselves in for the night, then listened while Dad read *Watership Down* aloud by lantern light.

Our kids enjoyed backyard camping so much that, when they were older, they would pitch a tent under our trees the first of June and sleep outside all summer long.

-22-
Plan & Save

Can't afford to take your dream vacation right away? Start planning for it, anyway!

Research shows that we get even more pleasure out of planning a trip than we do taking it. According to a study published in *Applied Research in Quality of Life* in 2010, the biggest boost to our happiness comes not from the vacation itself, but from the anticipation we experience before we ever leave home. Isn't that wild?

And it's all the more reason to share the love and involve your family during the trip planning phase. Discuss together where you'd like to travel and what you'd want to do. Then brainstorm ways to make those dreams a reality.

- Collect loose change in a coin jar for the vacation fund
- Hold a garage sale and set aside your earnings for travel
- Gather recyclables and put the money you get toward the trip
- Set up an automatic draw on your paycheck to go into vacation savings

-25-
Pack Per Day

B efore we took a second road trip, my husband surprised me by investing in three brand new sets of matching, monogrammed luggage. Twenty years later, we're still wheeling those things all over God's creation.

Still, organizing our clothes by day instead of by person had worked so well with the paper bags that I've continued to pack that way, suitcases or not.

For efficiency's sake, I bundle our clothes by wrapping each person's pants, socks, and underwear inside the day's shirt. Since we usually try to coordinate the colors we wear while traveling (refer to Chapter 27), this means I end up with one stack of red outfits for everyone, another of green, another of navy, and so forth.

Our suitcases are large enough that I can usually fit two or three days' worth of clothes into each one, depending on how many kids are tagging along and in what season of the year we're traveling (winter wear is so much bulkier than summer!)

Not only does packing this way eliminate the need to cart multiple bags into the hotel each night, but it also ensures kids have enough socks and underwear to last the whole trip.

-26-
Individual Backpacks

The only time our family makes an exception and forgoes our communal bag is when we're traveling overseas. We've backpacked Europe twice (see Chapter 69), and both times we put all our kids in charge of carrying their own clothes.

We used standard backpacks for the first trip, but that proved burdensome and tiring, especially for the younger children—*and for Mom!*

So on our return trip, we used backpacks that were equipped with wheels and extendable handles. Those things made a world of difference.

We could fit enough clothes for about ten days in each pack. But by wearing most of our outfits two days in a row and switching out layers, that was enough to last us almost three weeks.

An added bonus of traveling with carryon-sized packs was that we could get in and out of airports much more quickly. No checking bags before flights or waiting around afterward for our luggage to show up on the automated carousel. Plus, we were less likely to have bags lost, stolen, or delayed as we kept them in view the entire trip.

-27-
Color Coded Wardrobe

When our children were little, we would all dress in matching shirts whenever we took a trip or were likely to encounter a crowd. The consistent colors make it easier to count heads—something we spend an inordinate amount of time doing, especially when we're on a vacation.

Even today, you can pick up cotton-blend T-shirts on sale for $2 to $3 apiece at Hobby Lobby or Michael's. In the early years, I bought one of every color for each member of our family, then put them aside to use only when traveling. We'd wear red on Mondays, orange on Tuesdays, yellow on Wednesdays, green on Thursdays—and on down the line.

Not only did doing so make it easier to keep track of everybody, but it also made for brighter, more colorful pictures for our memory books and photo albums.

As the kids grew older and were less apt to wander off, we'd let them pick clothes out of their own closets to fit the day's color scheme: shades of blue one day, khaki and white the next, navy stripes the next, etc.

We're able to maintain a coordinated look this way while still allowing our kids to express their own sense of style. A win, for everyone!

-28-
To Wash or Not to Wash

Before leaving home, you'll need to decide whether or not you want to wash clothes while you're on vacation.

Saving it until you get home gives you a longer break from your routine chores, but also means you'll need to pack more clothes. And since it will all be dirty by the time you get back, you'll have your work cut out for you afterwards.

Nevertheless, I much prefer doing it this way rather than hunting down an out-of-town washeteria and spending half a day processing and repacking all our laundry.

If your accommodations are equipped with a washer and dryer, however, I'm all for doing laundry on the road. This set up offers several advantages:

- You can pack lighter—no need to fit a full week's worth of clothes into your suitcase
- Wash a load at night while everyone's asleep—no need to waste sightseeing time doing laundry
- No more dragging wet swimsuits from one hotel to the nest on road trips
- You'll have less to wash when you return home— most of your clothes will already be clean

-29-
A Sample Packing List

Although I'm usually the one who organizes everything into suitcases, I give each family member a list of what they'll need for a trip. They bring their clothes downstairs and stack them in laundry baskets (one for each person). This makes it easier on me when I'm ready to pack it. My packing list for a 5-day trip would look something like this:

- shirts x 5 (I normally specify color, too: navy; gray; lime or yellow; red plaid; blue or green stripes)
- shorts or jeans x 5
- underwear and socks x 5 pair
- swimsuit
- pajamas

I've always kept a family toiletry bag stocked and ready to go (see Chapter 30). But some of our older kids like to pack their own now and will put that in their basket, too. Additionally, I pack the following:

- my feather pillow (some kids bring pillows, too)
- phone and laptop computer & chargers
- books to read (aloud to family & silently to self)
- needlework (to do in the car)
- snacks for the road
- printed copies of itinerary + any coupons we need

-30-
Pre-Stocked Toiletries

As I mentioned in the last chapter, I keep our toiletry bag ready-to-go at all times, so I never have to worry about forgetting to pack a toothbrush or a razor.

I stock our little leather, double-zippered case with the following essentials:

- folding toothbrushes for everyone in the family, labeled by name
- a travel sized tube of toothpaste
- a tube of Blistex for chapped lips
- a small black comb
- a hairbrush (I packed a folding one until my husband surprised me with a brush shaped like a mermaid a few years back. Now that one is my travel brush ☺)
- extra ponytail elastics
- a razor and travel sized shaving cream
- a full-sized antiperspirant
- nail-clippers
- a neutral shade of nail polish
- a small bottle of eye drops (for husband's allergies)
- ear drops (to use after swimming)
- a small first aid kit (see Chapter 101)

Section 5

On the Road Again

-31-
Pray First

Our family begins every road trip with prayer. Before we ever pull out of the driveway back home, we all bow heads and ask God's blessing on our time away:

- We ask Him to keep us safe on the road and protect us from harm
- We ask Him to keep us well
- We ask Him to watch over our house and any family members remaining at home while we're away
- We pray for clear weather
- We pray for patience with one another
- We ask Him to help us all get along (despite being cooped up in a car for long hours)
- We ask Him to help us have fun
- We pray we'd shine for Jesus to everyone we meet

Not only do we pray for ourselves, but we enlist the prayers of family and friends on our behalf. I'm convinced one of the main reasons most of our vacations go so smoothly is because I send a detailed itinerary to my mother before every trip, and she offers specific prayers for us every day.

Sometimes we even bring Nana along with us. Thankfully, she prays just as hard on the road as she does at home. ☺

-32-
Car Maintenance

It should probably go without saying, but you need to be sure your car is in good working order before you set out on a trip of any length. And don't keep driving if the engine light comes on!

That's a lesson we learned the hard way. We could have done *Disney* for what one weekend trip to Oklahoma cost us after we'd paid for a tow truck, taxi, car rental, gas, engine repair, and one-way plane ticket (so Doug could drive our van back home once it was working again).

So now we make sure we're not overdue for an oil change before we ever leave town. Ideally, you should service your car a day or two in advance of your trip. Check tire pressure and tread, too.

If you forget, you can always do what we've done more times than I care to remember: You can load all of your luggage, snacks, and children into the car, pull out of your driveway (after prayers!), and tack an extra 30-minutes onto your already long day of driving by stopping at Jiffy-Lube on your way out of town.

It's a hassle, yes. But it sure beats breaking down on the side of the road!

-33-
AAA—for Peace of Mind

Sometimes, even when you've been careful to check your tires and service your car and switch out the oil before hitting the road, unforeseen problems still crop up.

Like hitting a patch of ice and winding up in a snowbank. Or running out of gas miles from the nearest station. Or locking your keys inside your car—maybe even with the engine running and a baby or two strapped into their car seats!

In times like these, an American Automobile Association membership has been worth its weight in gold.

Over the years, AAA has come to our rescue more times than I can count. They've pulled us out of ditches. Put gas in our tanks. Towed us to repair shops. Reunited us with keys, purses, and toddlers.

In Texas, the basic AAA membership costs $55 a year—a small price to pay for peace of mind. And with the discounts AAA offers on hotels, dining, and other attractions, we end up saving more money than we spend in annual dues.

Plus, members can request free copies of AAA TourBooks, a great source for vacation inspiration, organized by state!

-34-
Break It Up

We have friends who power straight through road trips, driving 18 hours at a lick with nary a stop except the occasional bathroom break. I guess that's one good way to make the family grateful (read: *relieved!)* when travel time is over and the vacation can officially begin.

Our family tends toward the opposite extreme. We spend days and days getting to where we're going—far longer than is really necessary.

That's because, in our minds, the car ride is as much a part of the vacation as our final destination. We may not spend as much time at the end of the line, but I daresay we enjoy the journey a lot more than our direct-driving friends.

Whether you favor lengthy drives or frequent stops, I hope you'll break up your travel time at least a little bit. Pull over every three to four hours for the sake of everybody's health and sanity.

Stretch you legs. Drink some water. Empty your bladder. Grab a snack. Get some air. Smell the roses.

Unless, of course, the baby is sleeping. Then you should try to get as far down the road as possible. ☺

-35-
Memorize the Map

Once, back when my husband was in medical school, he found himself in an elevator with a woman he instantly recognized from something he'd read in the school paper. So he struck up a conversation with her.

Alarmed that a perfect stranger was so familiar with her background—where she'd gone to school, what she'd studied, different awards she'd won—she asked how he knew so much about her. "From that article the paper printed welcoming you to town," he explained. She waited until the elevator reached her floor, then told him as she stepped out, "That article was published *seven years ago.*"

All this to say, my husband was blessed with an amazing memory. He could easily pass a test on information he read a single time. He could spot a phone number on a billboard and recall it weeks later. And he could study a map before we left home and drive us straight to our destination.

But that was in the era before smart phones. Now when we travel, he feels compelled to consult Google maps every ten minutes. Can you relate? Whether you memorize the map or depend on your GPS, *keep your eyes on the road while driving!* If you need to look up directions or type an address into your phone, either pull over or have a passenger do it.

-36-
Are We There Yet?

Even an only child can drive his parents crazy with constant requests for status reports: *Are we there yet?* But multiply that by twelve, and you have a real recipe for parental insanity.

I remember taking one trip with all our youngsters when they started peppering us with *are-we-almost-theres* before we'd even made it out of our own hometown. So my husband struck a bargain with them. He'd give a quarter to everyone who refrained from asking that question for the duration of our trip.

We enjoyed a 30-minute respite before our oldest daughter rephrased the inquiry: *Have we almost earned our quarters yet?* Still, it gave us a little bit of a break. If you need one, too, make sure you have a few quarters in your pocket before you leave on your next trip.

-37-
Chart Your Progress

To help your children visualize the progress you're making toward your final destination (instead of asking "Is *that* where we're going?" every ten minutes), print out several maps of the area you'll be traversing.

Mark your chosen route, circling major cities or landmarks along the way, and give a copy to each of your children. That way, they can follow along while you go.

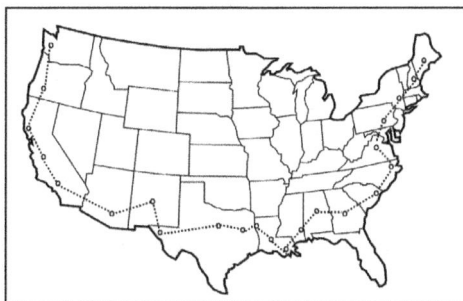

We did this the first year we traveled coast to coast. Not only did it help quell our children's curiosity as to how soon we might arrive at our final destination, but it also provided a great hands-on geography lesson.

Every time we crossed another state line or stopped for food, gas, or potty breaks, we'd break out our maps and mark our progress. The kids would use a marker to outline our route and color in the cities we'd already passed—like working a real-life dot-to-dot. Give it a try next time you have a long way to travel with inquisitive kids in the car.

-38-
Pit Stops

Whenever we stop on the road—for gas, food, or to let somebody use the restroom—we make sure *everyone* goes to the restroom, whether they think they need to or not.

We also take advantage of such breaks to check and change diapers, to nurse hungry babies, and to empty all the trash out of the van. By maximizing every stop we choose to make, we minimize the number of stops we have to make. At least, in theory.

My husband once took our son on a normally-four-and-a-half-hour road trip that took *eight* due to all the pit stops our 13-year old had to make.

Most teenagers don't notify their parents every time they use the restroom, so we had no idea how frequently our boy was urinating until he had to request bathroom breaks every 20 minutes on that car ride. Turns out, their little road trip may've saved our son's life, because it alerted us to the fact he had undiagnosed Type 1 diabetes. Had we not detected it when we did, he could have slipped into a coma *and died.*

Keep that in mind if you ever find yourself making more pit stops than normal: frequent urination, excessive hunger, and excessive thirst are all markers for diabetes. So check it out!

-39-
Stay Awake

One of my favorite songs out of *Mary Poppins* is the lullaby she sang to Jane and Michael:

> *Stay awake, don't rest your head.*
> *Don't lie down upon your bed.*
> *You're not sleepy, as you seem.*
> *Stay awake, don't nod or dream…*

Of course, Mary Poppins' admonitions were completely ineffectual, because the song lulled her charges right to sleep.

Unfortunately, driving affects me that same way. I can only make it 15-20 minutes behind the wheel before those parallel lane markers steadily rolling past put me in a trance.

Fortunately, my husband and most of my older children are immune to the hypnotic effect of sitting behind the steering wheel, so they do the majority of the driving. On those rare occasions when I can't avoid driving, I take a lot of stretch breaks.

If you're too sleepy to drive safely, you need to pull over, too. Driving while exhausted is just as dangerous as driving intoxicated. So run laps around the car. Do jumping jacks. Sing opera. Grab a cup of coffee. Stay awake. No nodding or dreaming when you're the one driving!

Section 6

Happy Diversions

-40-
Boredom Busters

Sometimes our kids pack a deck of cards for passing travel time or a magnetic travel game or perhaps even a pack of crayons and a coloring book.

The big kids usually bring a book or two to read on the road; little ones may tote along a pillow and blanket or a favorite stuffed animal.

Once when we toured the East Coast while studying early American history, I prepared notebooks for the kids full of maps and worksheets about each state we'd be traveling through.

The worksheets featured coloring pages of the official state flags, state birds, state seals, and other interesting information.

Mockingbird

TEXAS
- STATE PLEDGE -

"Honor the Texas flag:
I pledge allegiance
to thee, Texas,
one state under God,
one and indivisible."

You can visit our family web-site to download a FREE set of state bird coloring pages simply by following this link: *http://bit.ly/birdsbystate*

-41-
Audio Books

I originally entitled this chapter "Books on Tape." Even though we are several generations past cassette tapes now, I still think in those terms.

Whether you're using cassettes, CDs, MP3s, or just linking your smart phone to your car's sound system and listening that way, audio books make travel time fly. I vastly prefer them to videos, because you can still look out the windows and admire the countryside as you're listening to books much more easily than when you're watching movies.

It's also easy to hit pause and discuss what you've heard at the end of a chapter—or even during an especially thought-provoking passage.

Plus, you can pick topics that relate to your travels. We listened to *Johnny Tremain* on a trip to Boston, *Anne of Green Gables* while driving through Canada, *Sing Down the Moon* on a tour of the Southwest, and biographies of several presidents and other historical figures before visiting their homes.

-42-
Alphabet Game

The alphabet game is one of those family traditions I assumed everybody already knew about, but when I mentioned it a few summers ago to some friends from London, I was met with blank stares.

I had to explain how it's played, because the concept was completely new to them.

So, in case you are reading this and have likewise missed out on playing this popular travel game, here's what you do:

Everybody in the car begins at the same time. Search billboards, license plates, store fronts, road signs for the letters of the alphabet, in order. Anything outside your vehicle that has writing on it is fair game.

You can race each other to see who can finish first, or you may work as a team to complete this challenge together. But be forewarned! It's easy to get stuck on the letter Q— sometimes for half an hour or more.

In Texas, we have Dairy Queens and Quality Inns to help us out, but it may take a little longer to make it all the way from A to Z in other parts of the country!

-43-
Sing Alongs

Switch off the radio (or pause the audio book) for awhile and make a little music of your own. Sing alongs are fun, whether you can carry a tune or not.

Our family loves singing Christmas carols in the car (even in the heat of the summer!), as well as old hymns and praise choruses from church.

But we've also been known to sing silly songs like "One hundred Bottles of Pop on the Wall" (*100 bottles of pop! Take one down, pass it around, 99 bottles of pop on the wall!*). That one will keep you occupied for a bit. ☺

If you're really up for a challenge, try singing a song in rounds, with everybody starting in on the tune one stanza apart:

> *Row, row, row your boat*
> *Gently down a stream!*
> *Merrily, merrily, merrily, merrily!*
> *Life is but a dream.*

I don't know about life being a dream, but the Bible does tell us it's a vapor—here today, gone tomorrow. So let's use our time wisely and make some wonderful memories with our kids while we're still able to do so.

-44-
Brain Teasers

When I was in elementary school, my father hit on a great way to keep me quiet and happily occupied during long road trips.

He'd pose detailed logic problems for me to work in my head, such as this one:

> *You're lost in the jungle, trying to find your way back to port. The jungle is entirely populated by two tribes. One tribe always and only speaks the truth. The other tribe always and only tells lies. You come to a fork in the road, guarded by a native. You don't know whether he's a liar or a truth teller, and you can only ask him one yes-or-no question. How should you phrase your question so as to correctly identify which road will take you back to port?* *

Interestingly, one of the problems Dad gave me back when I was nine or ten, I didn't encounter again until I was doing my graduate work in mathematics. Fortunately, I still remembered his explanation of how to work it!

If you have kids who like to think, bring a book of brain teasers and quiz them on the road. It'll keep them quiet and will strengthen their brain muscles at the same time.

* Solution on p. 152

-45-
Hunting License Plates

Race to see who can spot the most license plates from other states. Can you find all fifty?

Like the alphabet game, this activity can be played alone or as a group. It helps to have an alphabetical list of all the states, so you can check them off as you go.

Or reinforce your geography lessons by printing some labeled U.S. maps, instead, and having your kids color in each state as they spy plates hailing from that locale.

STATE LICENSE PLATE GAME

Every time you spot a license plate from a particular state, check it off your list:

ALABAMA	MISSISSIPPI
ALASKA	MISSOURI
ARIZONA	MONTANA
ARKANSAS	NEBRASKA
CALIFORNIA	NEVADA
COLORADO	NEW HAMPSHIRE
CONNECTICUT	NEW JERSEY
DELAWARE	NEW MEXICO
FLORIDA	NEW YORK
GEORGIA	NORTH CAROLINA
HAWAII	NORTH DAKOTA
IDAHO	OHIO
ILLINOIS	OKLAHOMA
INDIANA	OREGON
IOWA	PENNSYLVANIA
KANSAS	RHODE ISLAND
KENTUCKY	SOUTH CAROLINA
LOUISIANA	SOUTH DAKOTA
MAINE	TENNESSEE
MARYLAND	TEXAS
MASSACHUSETTS	UTAH
MICHIGAN	VERMONT
MINNESOTA	VIRGINIA
	WASHINGTON
	WEST VIRGINIA
	WISCONSIN
	WYOMING

© 2019 - www.flandersfamily.info

Use one map or list if you are working together as a team, or print a separate sheet for each person if you want to compete against each other.

To download a printable game board visit our free printables page at *www.flandersfamily.info.*

60

-46-
Sticker Books

Several years ago, we stumbled upon a wonderful travel activity for our craft-loving children: *Paint by Sticker* books.

These books contain very intricate designs, each with numbered sections that correspond to a solid colored sticker cut in the precise shape needed to fill it.

The designs are fun to complete, and the results are bold, bright, and beautiful. Some of them turned out good enough to frame, and my kids have even won a couple of blue ribbons for their completed designs in the Creative Arts Competition at the State Fair.

Most of the paint-by-sticker books we own are centered around a theme: birds, fish, zoo animals, famous works of art, travel posters, etc.

With as many as 200 tiny stickers per design, each page will keep your children engrossed for an hour or so.

Ours use them to keep their hands busy while their minds are engaged listening to audio books on the road.

-47-
Counting Cars

I'm not sure where my kids learned it, but for a while, every time they spotted a Volkswagen Beetle, they'd yell "Slug Bug!" and punch their nearest sibling in the shoulder.

They'd do this in a playful way, but it still drove me and my husband crazy, so we eventually outlawed that game. (We suggested they could play "Hug Bug" instead, but that one never caught on. Ha!)

Our children also snap at Mustangs. I think one of our daughters-in-law taught them that game.

When I was growing up, my family played a car game that involved neither slugging nor snapping.

We'd each choose a color, then would race to see who could find the most cars that matched the color they picked in a specified amount of time—usually ten minutes or so.

I can tell you right now that, nine times out of ten, black or white will win the game. But it's much more fun to count red or yellow or green cars— in my humble opinion!

62

-48-
Travel Bingo

For many years, we had reusable bingo cards we'd pull out on long road trips.

The squares contained little pictures of things like traffic lights and school busses and gas stations. They also came equipped with tiny, sliding red doors you could close over the pictures as you spotted them along the way.

I don't know what ever happened to our little cardboard bingo cards, or if they are even still available for purchase today. But you can visit our family website's free printable page and download the files for five different bingo cards like the one pictured here.

If you'll laminate a copy for each family member, you can use a dry erase pen to mark them and reuse them indefinitely.

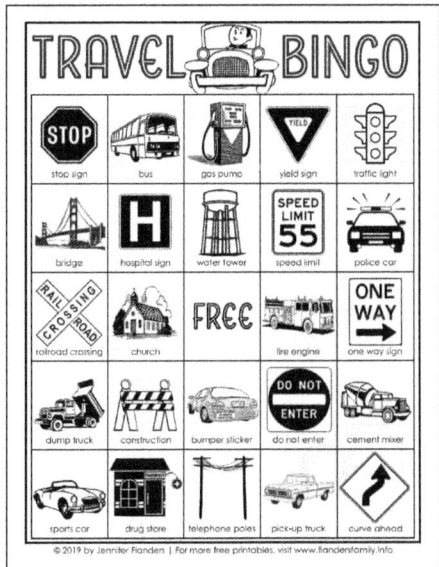

63

-49-
Hangman

If you get tired of playing tic-tac-toe and connect-the-dots, Hangman is another fun pen-and-paper game good for long car rides.

It's played like *Wheel of Fortune,* only it uses gallows instead of a buzzer.

One person chooses a word or phrase and writes down the appropriate number of blanks to spell it out. Other players take turns guessing the letters one at a time.

If the guessed letter appears in the phrase, the hangman puts it in all the appropriate places and the player who guessed it gets another turn.

Otherwise, the hangman adds a body part to the gallows (head, body, arms, or legs) and the next player takes a turn.

If you can't correctly guess the phrase before a whole body is hanging on the gallows, you lose!

I HOP_ _OU HAV_ A
FU_ TIM_ PLA_I_G
HA_GMA_ !

-50-
Twenty Questions

nother fun game to play when traveling is *20 Questions*. One person thinks of something, and everyone else takes turns asking questions and trying to figure out what it is.

Anybody who guesses correctly within the cumulative 20-question limit wins and gets to think up something for the next round.

Otherwise, the original player conjures up another mental image, and the question count resets at zero.

One last thing: you have to be careful to phrase your questions in such a way as to elicit a "yes" or "no" response. Otherwise, you'll lose a question without getting an answer.

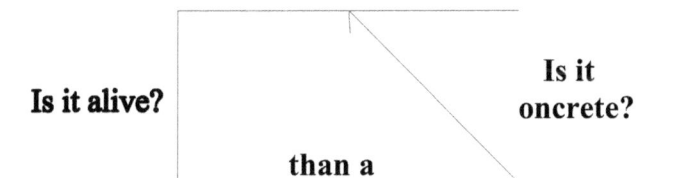

Is it alive?

Is it oncrete?

than a

Section 7

A Lifestyle of Learning

-51-
Extended Field Trips

Since our family homeschools, we view our vacations more like extended field trips. Whenever possible, we spend time before we go studying things related to the locales we plan to visit: the history, the landscape, the culture, the sights we're likely to see along the way.

Prior knowledge of an area deepens the memories we make once we arrive. And it also helps us to catalogue new information in our minds, as we notice similarities and differences between various places we visit.

Preparing for our travels and taking the time to learn something about our destination beforehand is just one more way of increasing our anticipation of a trip (which we know from Chapter 22 also increases our overall enjoyment).

But we don't stop with this preparatory period of study. We also try to pack as much educational value as possible into the trips themselves.

Like you, we want our children to love learning, so in this section, I'm sharing some of our best ideas for incorporating educational opportunities into your next vacation. Feel free to pick and choose the activities that appeal most to your family. It would be hard to fit them all into a single trip.

-52-
Factory Tours

Factory tours are one of our family's favorite things to do on vacation. They're one of the biggest reasons we prefer driving to flying, because it allows us to stop all along the way and learn about how stuff is made.

The opportunity to view behind-the-scenes manufacturing operations keeps us learning, even while we're on holiday. You seldom have to fight crowds on a factory tour, and many businesses offer them for free. (For a good sampling of available tours, searchable by state, check out the website *factorytoursusa.com*.)

Try it, and you'll be hooked. That's because factory tours are inspiring! From carving granite to blowing glass to cultivating tea to manufacturing guitars to mining salt, there is a certain level of craftsmanship that goes into creating even the most mundane items.

Observing the many steps required to make such things is simultaneously humbling and motivating. It fosters a deeper appreciation for the world around us and the workers in it.

Factory tours make for far more interesting rest stops than gas stations (and the bathrooms are usually cleaner, too)!

-53-
Science & Technology

We normally buy an annual membership to our local science museum. Not only does this give our family unlimited visits all year long, but membership grants us free admission to hundreds of science museums across the country.

It's a great way to support your own community, and is a fantastic deal for families who love to travel. This is especially true for families with as many kids as we have.

Although some museums now restrict the number of kids allowed in on a family membership, for most of our children's growing up years that wasn't the case. The majority of museums placed no limits on family size; a family membership covered admission for both parents plus all children under 18 living in the same household.

You can find a list of currently participating museums at the Association of Science and Technology Centers website (*https://www.astc.org/passport/*). Almost every trip we take includes a free visit to at least one museum on this list. They are all different, and our kids have had a blast and learned a lot exploring the scores of science and technology museums we've visited so far with our membership card!

-54-
Off the Beaten Path

We don't buy an annual membership to a garden listed with the American Horticultural Society every year, but we do occasionally join the Dallas Arboretum or Garvan Woodland Gardens.

On years that either of those memberships are current, I check their reciprocity lists when planning vacations, so as to get the most of our membership.

Many cities (like ours) have beautiful parks and gardens that are free and open to the public. I'd love to have a state-by-state listing of those places, but have yet to find one online. If you know of one, please send me the link!

Meanwhile, try visiting the American Horticultural Society website at *https://www.ahsgardening.org/*. Go to the directory tab and click through to an individual garden's website to determine admission policies. Note that most of the gardens labeled "free admission" on the master list means free *reciprocal admission* for AHS arboretum members, not necessarily free for everybody.

-55-
Junior Rangers

The Junior Ranger program is one of the best-kept secrets I've ever stumbled upon. I can't believe how many National Parks I've visited, both as a child and as an adult, without realizing this program was even available.

But now that I *do* know, our kids have collected scores of badges, patches, and certificates for participating.

Requirements vary from park to park, but normally children must complete several pages/activities in a short workbook to earn their award. The activities are fun and easy, and the workbooks are usually FREE (although we've visited one or two parks that charged a buck or two to cover printing costs). For more details and a list of participating parks—plus information on how you can earn even more badges at home—visit *https://www.nps.gov/kids/jrRangers.cfm* .

If you happen to have a fourth grader at home, your entire family can visit any of our National Parks for free, all year long. Check it out here: *https://www.nationalparks.org/our-work/campaigns-initiatives/every-kid-park*. You'll find great museums, educational videos, and interactive exhibits in each park's visitors center. So check the National Park Service website to see what parks may be near you or your next vacation destination (or en route)!

-56-
Visit the Library

Our family loves to read. So it makes sense that we spent a lot of time in the library when our kids were growing up—sometimes even when we were on vacation.

While we don't normally borrow books from out-of-town libraries, we do like browsing their shelves and participating in their community events.

If you have young children, don't overlook public libraries as a source of free fun while you're traveling. Check the calendar of events for libraries in the area you plan to visit. Many of them sponsor weekly story times, summer movies, special speakers, 3-D printers, craft programs, dance classes, maker spaces, author events, and book clubs, as well as meet-ups for Lego lovers and American Doll fans.

Some libraries are impressive just because of their historical significance. The US Library of Congress in Washington, DC, is a must-see for that reason, as is the New York Public Library next to Bryant Park.

Our family also enjoyed the Burton Barr Central Library in Phoenix, Arizona, for its cool architecture.

-57-
Free Museum Days

We've found that lots of museums in big cities offer free admission one day a month—and sometimes even one evening a week.

If your travel plans are flexible, it's worth checking to see if any of the museums you're interested in visiting offer open houses or free days or other community events.

A good place to find such information is on the museum website. Check their online calendar of events, search for "family specials," or simply call the museum directly. It never hurts to ask.

The only drawback of free days is that you'll probably end up sharing the museum with a larger throng of people. This may not be a problem at art museums, but can get a little hairy at children's museums when you're trying to keep tabs on several kids at once who've vanished into a mob.

Thankfully, if you do much of your traveling off-season, like we do, the free day crowds are still smaller than peak-season masses that flock to the museums every day during the summer.

-58-
Community Events

Even if none of the museums in the area offer free days while you're in town, there may be other free events you can enjoy while you're there. To find them, check the events calendar at the city's chamber of commerce. You can often find this information online.

Both in our own hometown and on the road, we've enjoyed a wide variety of FREE events found through public notices and events calendars, including:

- movies in the park
- Rose Festival events
- craft bazaars
- rock and mineral shows
- spring flower trails
- open houses
- history lectures
- Civil War re-enactments
- ballet performances
- Shakespeare festivals and performances
- puppet shows
- car shows
- symphonies under the stars
- and Christmas festivities of every imaginable sort!

-59-
Have Costumes/ Will Travel

Just like stereotypical homeschoolers, we have an entire closet full of period costumes. And we love any excuse to wear them. We've donned tabards and chainmail for Renaissance festivals, waistcoats and doublets at Plymouth Plantation, colonial outfits in Historic Williamsburg, and antebellum gowns and Civil War uniforms at Gettysburg.

Dressing for the era we're studying really helps history come alive. So we do it every chance we get. Most of the time, we receive a warm welcome for our efforts, but on a couple of occasions, it has backfired.

When we dressed in first century tunics and robes to go to the Holy Land Experience in Florida, we were turned away until we changed back into our street clothes. It seems they had a policy against patrons wearing costumes. (Disney theme parks have the same rule for guests older than 14.)

I also packed our colonial costumes for us to wear in Old Salem, which we did, convinced we would blend right in, which we didn't. We could count on one hand the number of costumed interpreters we met during our off-season visit, and even *they* regarded us with puzzled expressions and asked loaded questions about our religious background, which they presumed must be very strict, indeed!

-60-
Living History

Even if you have no desire to dress in period costumes yourself, "living history" museums make for some wonderfully educational outings.

Often the docents at these historical sites are themselves costumed interpreters. As they conduct your tour, they'll transport you back in time and give you a better idea of what it was like to live in the period represented. What's more, they're usually very knowledgeable and enthusiastic history buffs who welcome thoughtful questions, so you can learn a lot from them if you have time to pick their brains.

Places like Colonial Williamsburg or Plymouth Plantation have costumed interpreters onsite every day. These locations are so big, they take a full day (or more) to fully explore. Other sites are smaller and may only have costumed guides available on the weekends or during special events. Good places to look for this kind of experience are military outposts, forts, pioneer villages, and similar historical settlements. You can find a partial listing organized by state on Wikipedia: *https://en.wikipedia.org/wiki/List_of_open-air_and_living_history_museums_in_the_United_States*.

You can tour state capitol buildings for free, too—those also make interesting historical stops.

- 61 -
Rest in Peace

I remember driving past a cemetery once when I was a little girl. My uncle, who was in the car at the time, pointed it out to me. "See that place?" he quipped. "People are just dying to go there!"

He was joking, of course, in a punny sort of way. However, I believe cemeteries and memorial parks do hold a certain attraction. Just think of the rows upon rows of crosses at Arlington National Cemetery. Or the somber battlegrounds and stately monuments at military parks like Gettysburg or Vicksburg.

One of my favorite free stops in Los Angeles is Forest Lawn Memorial Park. The Glendale site offers several points of interest, including a beautiful 15-ft by 30-ft stained glass recreation of Leonardo da Vinci's *The Last Supper* and a massive historical painting of *The Crucifixion* by Polish artist Jan Styka that measures 195 feet long and 45 feet tall.

They also have a beautiful museum and mausoleum, filled with marble and bronze statuary, including a life-size reproduction of Michelangelo's *Pieta*. We enjoyed visiting even with very young children. If you go, just remind your kids to be quiet and respectful while you're there—no running, yelling, or rowdy play allowed!

Section 8

Grab Some Grub on the Go

-62-
Healthy Snacks

Although pre-packaged snack foods are convenient, they're normally aren't very nutritionally dense. Looking for more healthful options to eat on the road? Consider packing a few of these options:

- grapes
- apples
- roasted chickpeas
- sugar snap peas & humus
- carrot & celery sticks
- pistachio nuts or almonds
- strawberries, blackberries, or blueberries
- Clementine oranges
- lightly salted popcorn
- trail mix
- fresh cherries
- toasted coconut
- bananas
- tomato juice

We've eaten all of these treats while traveling, although I try to stick with less messy things like nuts, carrots, and popcorn in the car, and save the stuff that might stain (blueberries, cherries, tomato juice) to pass out at rest stops.

-63-
Kids Eat Free

Go easy on the cook *and* on the checkbook! Check to see if your destination has any national chains that offer free kids' meals on certain days of the week (or search "kids eat free" plus the name of the city you're visiting). These Free Kid's Meal programs may end without notice, so be sure to call first to verify that kids (still) eat free.

- Bennigan's: Tuesday after 4PM (ages ≤12)
- Black-Eyed Pea: Tuesday after 4PM (ages ≤12)
- Corner Bakery: Tuesday after 4PM (ages ≤10)
- Denny's: Tue. & Sat. after 4PM (ages ≤10)
- Dickey's Barbecue: all day Sunday (ages ≤12)
- GattiTown Pizza: Mon. & Wed. after 5PM (ages ≤10)
- IHOP: Tuesday & Thursday after 4PM (ages ≤11)
- Jersey Mike's Subs: all day Sunday (ages ≤12)
- Luby's Cafeteria: Wed. & Sat. after 4PM (ages ≤10)
- Marie Callender's: all day Tue. & Sat. (ages ≤12)
- Rotolo's Pizza: Monday after 5PM (ages ≤12)
- Salsarita's: Saturday after 5PM (ages ≤12)
- Steak-n-Shake: all day Sat. & Sun. (ages ≤13)
- Texas Roadhouse: Tuesday after 4PM (ages ≤12)
- Tony Roma's: all day Sunday (ages ≤12.)

-64-
AAdvantage Dining

Of course, you have to eat while you're on vacation. Make those meals count by dining at restaurants that will award you with airline miles, as well. We typically earn 5 miles per dollar spent, but we sometimes get double that rate during special promotions.

To check your next vacation destination for participating restaurants, go to *https://aa.rewardsnetwork.com* and type in the name or zip code of the city you plan to visit. You can see the results in a list or—my favorite—view them on a map. That makes it super easy to locate something nearby when you're on the road.

To earn the points, you'll have to pay for your meal with a credit card. But any card will do (it needn't be a AAdvantage Reward card). Just make sure you've registered the card with the AAdvantage Dining program in advance.

Doing so is a one-time process. Once it is done, you never have to think about it again. Nor do you need to tell your waiter you're participating in the program. Miles are awarded automatically. Our family has even earned miles eating at restaurants we didn't know were in the program until we saw the miles post to our account a few days later.

-65-
Restaurant.com

We love eating at mom-and-pop joints, and many of the restaurants we find through *www.restaurant.com* definitely have that vibe. What makes them even better, though, is that they offer drastically reduced gift certificates through this program.

Customers must normally pay $10 for a $25 gift card, but I'd recommend signing up for Restaurant.com's mailing list and waiting for a sale. Every four to six weeks, they run a special where you can pick up all the $25 certificates you want for as little as $2 apiece. That's what I call a great deal!

Certificates never expire and can be be exchanged between restaurants if something keeps you from going to your original choice (as has sometimes happened to us when our travel plans have changed unexpectedly).

To locate participating restaurants, simply search by city or zip code on the website. For additional savings, you can go through *www.rakuten.com* (formerly known as Ebates) to buy your certificates and/or cross reference the Restaurant.com and AAdvantage Dining lists to find restaurants that participate in both programs. :-)

-66-
Go Grocery Shopping

Several grocery stores in my hometown now offer pickup service, and I'm hooked. Talk about a time saver! Have you tried it?

You do all the shopping online. No navigating heavy carts through crowded aisles trying to keep your kids from grabbing stuff that isn't on the list, in the budget, or good for anybody's diet.

Once your virtual cart is loaded, simply check out, schedule a pick-up time, and wait for a reminder text telling you your order is ready. They'll bring the groceries straight to your car and even load them into your trunk—all for free.

If you do your grocery shopping online at a national chain like Walmart, you can pick up supplies on vacation just as easily as you can at home. Just specify a pick-up location close to wherever you're staying. (Be sure to change the pick-up store back to the one you normally shop at, so you won't accidentally order from an out-of-town store once you get back home.)

87

-67-
Pack a Picnic

If the weather is nice, why not plan a picnic while you're on vacation? You can bring food from home in an ice chest to eat at a rest stop along the way.

Or you can wait and find a place to picnic once you arrive at your destination. Pick up fresh fruit and sandwich fixings from a local grocery store (or order them online for pick up), or swing through Chick-fil-A and grab some nuggets and lemonade.

Do a little research to see what kind of public gardens, parks, or picnic pavilions are available to you. If your kids are young, you may be able to choose one with a playground or splash pad.

Picnic tables are nice, but in their absence, you can spread a quilt or blanket on the ground and sit there to enjoy your fare. Just be sure to pack one in the car before you leave home.

-68-
Bring the Crockpot

A nother way to save dramatically on your food costs is take a crockpot along with you when you travel. You can put your dinner in to cook before leaving your room in the morning and come back to a hot meal that evening.

If the place where you're staying is equipped with a full kitchen, so much the better. If not, bring along some paper plates and disposable utensils to make clean up quick and easy.

You might even cook ahead and freeze a few meals in gallon zip-lock bags to bring along in an ice chest. They'll keep that way for several days, and preparing dinner will be as easy as sliding the contents into the crockpot when you're ready to prepare them.

One of our vehicles came equipped with a three-pronged outlet, we've even put foil-wrapped ham-n-cheese sandwich rolls in to warm while we're on the road. They smelled so good! Our mouths were watering long before we finally pulled over to eat them!

Section 9

Extra Savings

-69-
Frequent Flyer Miles

Although our family doesn't travel by plane frequently, we've used America Airlines "frequent flyer" miles to fly 8-11 people to Europe for FREE three times now.

Interested? It's not as hard as you think. Simply register for the programs listed below, then wait and watch your miles add up over time:

1. American AAdvantage—first, sign up at AA for an awards account, so you can start accumulating miles
2. AA Credit Cards—earn miles on credit purchases, plus bonus miles, just for signing up
3. AAdvantage Dining—see Chapter 64 to learn how to earn 5 miles per every dollar spent eating out
4. Strategic Shopping—use the AAdvantage eShopping portal to earn miles on online purchases
5. Energy Rewards—earn airline miles for your energy usage, plus bonus miles when you switch providers
6. Hotel Miles—see Chapter 70 for tips on earning miles when you stay at most national hotel chains

Earning miles is easy, so give it a try. Just by doing #2 and #5 above, you can usually earn enough miles for one round-trip ticket in the continental US, almost instantaneously!

-70-
Hotel Points

Virtually every hotel in America has some sort of customer loyalty program. Most are free to join, and you'll earn points every stay, which can be redeemed for free nights and other perks.

Some programs even allow guests to "double dip" by awarding points *and* miles each time you stay at one of their hotels. Others allow you to exchange points for miles.

There's no advantage to joining loyalty programs for hotels you never use, but you'll miss out if you stay at any brands associated with the following chains without first signing up for their membership awards:

- Choice Privileges - *https://www.choicehotels.com*
- Drury Rewards - *https://www.druryhotels.com/druryrewards*
- Hilton Honors - *https://hiltonhonors3.hilton.com*
- Hyatt Gold Passport - *https://world.hyatt.com*
- Intercontinental Hotel Group - *www.ihg.com/rewardsclub*
- Marriot BonVoy - *https://www.marriott.com/loyalty.mi*
- Radisson Rewards - *https://www.radissonrewards.com*
- Wyndam Rewards - *https://www.wyndhamhotels.com/wyndham-rewards*

-71-
Groupon Deals

I used to get frustrated with the Groupon site, as it seemed to mainly list offers that were of no interest to me. Then I learned how to use the site's search bar!

Just plug in the city you're visiting and search for "Things to Do." That will sufficiently narrow the results so that you don't have to wade through pages of stuff you don't want to find something you do.

The couple of minutes it takes to scan the relative offers really pays off! For instance, it got our entire family half-price admission to Wonder Works last time we were in Myrtle Beach—a substantial savings for our big crew!

We have saved as much as 70% off tickets to the Horse Park in Kentucky, rock climbing in Nevada, dinner shows in Tennessee, and world-class museums in Missouri.

We've also used Groupon deals to go bowling, go-karting, zorbing, and indoor skydiving.

You can find bargains on both fine and fast food dining through Groupon, as well—sometimes earning as much as 25% cashback on your meal at no extra cost. Just click a button to register for the special, and you're good to go.

-72-
Reciprocal Benefits

M any zoos, gardens, museums, and historical societies offer membership benefits that can save money for a family who loves to travel.

Our family visits our local zoo and science museum often enough to justify buying an annual membership to each. But reciprocal benefits make those memberships an even better bargain, because they get us free or discounted admission to hundreds of zoos and science centers all across the country —a perk we definitely make good use of when we travel!

Lots of other organizations offer similar benefits. Depending on when, where, and how often you travel, you might consider getting a membership or annual pass to any of the following organizations (though I'd probably stagger these memberships and not join them all in one year ☺):

- State or National Park Pass
- Children's Museum Membership
- Historical Museum Membership
- Sea World or Aquarium Pass
- City Pass (for discounts to various attractions)
- Arboretum or Botanical Garden Pass
- Membership to Six Flags or Legoland, etc.

-73-
Special Discounts

When considering ways to save money on vacations, don't overlook your various group memberships and affiliations. As I mentioned in Chapter 33, flashing a AAA card will save you money on hotel and attraction costs, but you can take advantage of similar savings with any of the following affiliations:

US MILITARY—lots of places offer free or reduced admission to active or retired military personnel. While my husband was active with the Army Reserves, we saved 70% off rack rates at some hotels. Even now, his veteran status got our family four free tickets to SeaWorld last year, thanks to their *Waves of Honor* program.

SENIOR CITIZENS—people as young as 50 are eligible for AARP membership and the discounts that come with it. But even without an AARP card, your advancing years may get you special pricing, so always be sure to ask!

HOMESCHOOLERS—if you belong to a local homeschool support group, you may qualify for additional discounts. We saved a bundle at Legoland and Colonial Williamsburg by flashing our Home School Legal Defense Association card. Even some retail stores (including Barnes&Noble, Half-Price Books, and JoAnn Fabric) extend educator discounts to homeschool teachers.

-74-
Off-Season Savings

Another benefit of homeschooling is the flexibility it affords to travel off-season. Not only do you have a lot of attractions all to yourselves that way, but the prices are often a fraction of what they cost during the high season.

We've scored some awesome deals over the years by traveling while everyone else is in school. But you don't have to homeschool to enjoy the perks of off-season travel.

If your children aren't old enough to go to school yet (or can miss a class for a week without hurting their grades)—and/or if you're retired or work remotely, you can take advantage of low-season specials, as well.

Instead of heading to the beach in the summer and to the mountains during ski season, turn it around. Build sandcastles while the rest of the world is snow skiing and hike mountain trails while everyone else is working on their tans.

You'll not only save money, but you won't have to fight the crowds, either.

-75-
The More the Merrier

I know it's a rarity to have 12 children in one family these days, but if even if you have just two or three times the national average, you may qualify for quantity discounts.

That was a recurrent theme in the classic story, *Cheaper by the Dozen*. The title came from the fact that Frank Gilbreth used that phrase liberally when negotiating group pricing for his sizable clan. *"Do my little Irishmen come cheaper by the dozen?"* he'd intone while proudly pointing to his progeny and finagling discounts on everything from ice cream cones to tonsillectomies.

Your family may never need a dozen sets of tonsils removed at once, but you probably would appreciate getting a price break on tours and attractions. So check to see what kind of specials they offer.

Some family discounts cover two parents and as many children as still live at home—a substantial savings over buying individual tickets (and a fantastic bargain for families as big as mine or the Gilbreths')!

99

Section 10

Home Away from Home

-76-
Affordable Lodging

Although sites like Expedia.com and Travelocity make it easy to compare hotel costs in a given area, I normally prefer booking our rooms directly with the hotel. Otherwise, I loose the hotel points and/or airline miles I would normally get with my stay. Plus, if you find a better rate elsewhere for the same room, many chains will either match or undercut the price.

Remember to join the rewards program (see Chapter 70) for every hotel you use, especially if you travel much. The points really add up! We recently got four free nights in New Orleans with points we'd earned from prior travels. Some rewards programs will even convert points to cash, which is always a welcome benefit.

While reservations can be made quickly and easily online, sometimes it's preferable to call and make the reservation directly by phone. This is especially true when traveling with lots of children.

I once read that you must ask three times to get their best rate. I'd do so routinely whenever I made a reservation by phone. It almost always paid off—sometimes significantly: *How much for a room? Do you have a AAA rate? Are you running any specials that would give me a better deal?*

-77-
Lots of Choices

Our strategy for vacation lodging has changed a lot over the years. What made sense when traveling with two kids doesn't when traveling with twelve, and vice versa.

Renting a house for a full week is usually more economical than booking three separate hotel rooms (as fire codes often require a party of our size to do) each night for seven nights.

But week-long rentals aren't as practical when you're making a cross-country road trip and only need a place to crash one night at a time.

With the exception of pitching tents for weeklong camping trips, most of our family vacations have been of the road trip variety with only one or two nights at each stop.

Here's a rundown of our favorite places to stay at each stage along the way (which I'll discuss further in the next few chapters):

- 0-2 kids—stay with relatives whenever possible
- 3-4 kids—book standard room at economy hotel
- 5-6 kids—stay in hotel suites or family rooms
- 7-9 kids—book two rooms or airbnb condominium
- 10 or more kids—join a vacation club ☺

-78-
Visit Relatives

Back when Doug and I were just starting out, our family was small and our bank account even smaller.

We lived on school loans for the first several years of our marriage, and the only traveling we did was to visit out-of-town relatives, who graciously put us up in their spare bedrooms for the couple of nights we were there.

That works well when your children are small, provided you watch them closely, keep them quiet, clean up their messes, and don't stay too long. ☺

If you're traveling to a city where no friend or family lives, check out *airbnb.com*. That site wasn't around when we were newly married, but our family used a similar service when backpacking Europe and found it to be an economical and enjoyable alternative to a traditional hotel stay.

-79-
Double Queens

Most standard hotel rooms will accommodate a maximum of four guests. You can sometimes talk them into five if one of the guests is a baby and you promise to bring a porta-crib from home (see Chapter 102), which is what we routinely did at that stage.

We'd always look for places that offered free breakfast and an indoor pool. That saved us the price of a meal and also provided a quick, fun way to freshen up after a long day of driving or sightseeing.

We still gravitate toward hotels with free breakfasts and all-season pools, although free Wi-Fi is important to us as well now.

When we had lots of little children and very limited funds, we stayed at one certain hotel chain almost exclusively any time we traveled, because they never asked how many children would be staying in the room with us when I'd call to book a reservation.

They offered delicious breakfasts, indoor pools, and (thanks to the don't-ask-don't-tell policy that was apparently in place at the time) we could bring sleeping bags from home and pack as many as six or seven of us into a single room.

-80-
Family Suites

As our family continued to grow, so did our children. The day soon came when couldn't comfortably fit all their bigger bodies into a single hotel room, so we started reserving two rooms.

It was also about this time that we discovered Embassy Suites. Although their rack rates were higher than we were accustomed to, they offered a great military discount of which we took full advantage during all the years my husband served in the Army Reserves. The first time I booked a room with them in St. Louis, military pricing dropped the room rate by more than 75%—for a spacious, two room suite with two double beds, a sofa sleeper, and a full, cooked-to-order breakfast.

We stuck with Embassy Suites as our family continued to grow, but eventually had to order two suites instead of just one to accommodate everybody. That doubled our cost... plus, once my husband finished his stint with the reserves, we no longer qualified for the military discount, so the price went up even further.

Several other hotels now offer reasonably-priced two-room suites, so if your family has outgrown a standard room, you may want to investigate this option.

-81-
A Place for Everything

Don't you hate it when you walk into a pristine hotel room with tidy beds and polished furniture, and within two minutes flat, it looks like a tornado struck it, with socks, shoes, wet swimsuits, and overflowing suitcases scattered all about the room?

Such messes can really interfere with the peace and calm we want to enjoy on vacation, so we trained our kids early to follow a few simple rules, which keep things tidy, no matter where we're staying.

Our first rule is that kids keep out of the family suitcase. Whenever it is time to change clothes, Mom distributes fresh ones to everyone. This way, the stacks of clean clothes in the suitcase stay neat and organized.

We also keep our toiletry bag on the bathroom counter next to the sink, but the contents remain zipped inside when we aren't using them. Not only does this keep the counter top tidy, but it also prevents our leaving toothbrushes, combs, and razors behind when we check out.

We use a collapsible tray to keep room keys, car keys, reading glasses, wallet, and watch together and accounted for (and high enough that little ones can't reach them).

-82-
Kick Off Your Shoes

At home, we keep shelves by our back door plus a big basket on the porch for collecting shoes.

That way, nobody tracks mud into the house or has to hunt a lost pair when it's time to go somewhere. Everyone's shoes are always right where we left them. Where they belong.

We employ a similar habit whenever we travel, which can be summed up with this simple reminder:

SHOES GO
IN THE BOTTOM DRAWER

Everyone down to our 2 year-old knows this rule, and we seldom have to remind them anymore. It's the first thing they do when we get to our room.

We use a dresser drawer for our shoes to keep crawling babies from chewing on them, but your family may prefer to line shoes up under the sink or put them in the floor of the closet. The important thing is just to have a clearly defined destination for everything, so it becomes second nature to put them where they go.

-83-
Dealing with Dirty Laundry

When traveling, we store our dirty clothes in dresser drawers, too. If three drawers are available, we'll put whites in the top drawer, darks in the middle, and shoes in the bottom.

Any jackets, nightgowns, or undergarments we plan to use again before laundering get hung up on hangers in the closet after their first wearing or folded and put in a safe place.

Swimwear falls into a category all its own. Our first rule here is: *No wet swimsuits on the beds!* It takes a while for all of us to get changed in and out of our swimsuits, and the suits are invariably damp when we have them on, if not dripping wet.

This rule keeps the bedclothes clean and dry. After a swim, we work fast to get everyone back into dry clothes, throwing the suits into a sink or tub while we're changing. Then, the older ones help Mom wring them out and hang them up to dry. If it bothers you to see wet suits draped over shower rods and towel racks, try laying a dry towel on the floor of the closet and hanging them neatly on hangers above. They stay out of sight that way and dry better, too!

-84-
More Bang for Your Buck

About the time our family grew so big that hotels began requiring us to reserve three or four rooms at once, we booked a preview weekend with a popular vacation club. In exchange for sitting through an hour-long sales pitch while we were there, we got an unbelievable rate on a 3-night stay.

We had previewed a different brand a decade earlier and really enjoyed it. But at that time, our family was smaller and didn't travel as much, so we had no trouble saying no when they tried to sell us the plan. In fact, when we heard the price tag for that particular line of resorts, we nearly laughed out loud. *Did they think money grows on trees?*

This time, my husband ran the numbers before we met with the sales rep. Once our negotiated price dropped below what we typically paid for lodging per year of travel, we signed on the dotted line. It has been a fantastic investment. The accommodations are spacious and come with a full kitchen, washer, and dryer in almost every unit. We have access to resorts all over the world. Plus, by traveling off-season, we're really able to maximize our points.

If you'd be interested in booking a preview weekend with our vacation club, we can arrange an invite. Just email your contact info to flandersfamily@flandersfamily.info.

-85-
Double-Check the Room

When it comes time to check out of your home-away-from-home accommodations, whatever form they take, it is always a good idea to make a final pass through the room to make sure nothing has been forgotten or accidentally left behind.

The routine our family follows is this: After breakfast, Mom packs everything up, piling our dirty clothes into the empty spaces left by the clean clothes in our suitcase. If we're mid-trip and our dirty clothes must share a bag with what remains of our clean stuff, I separate anything damp or stinky into a large zip-lock bag. (Or, in a pinch, I'll use one of those plastic laundry bags the hotel provides.)

Once everything's repacked and the luggage is moved into the hall, Dad searches the closets, drawers, and bedclothes for anything the rest of us missed. Occasionally, he even finds something. ☺

Doug then settles our accounts at the front desk and turns in our room keys while the kids and I wheel our bag(s) to the van to load everybody/everything up. Then we say a quick prayer to ask for God's continued protection, and we're on the road again!

112

Section 11

Savvy Souvenirs

-86-
Minimalist Mementos

L ittle children love bringing home things to help them remember the places they've gone.

But while I understand the urge (because I'm sentimental, too), I don't like to see them spend a lot of money on junk that is going to break in five minutes or languish, forgotten, in the bottom of an already overstuffed drawer.

And so we gravitate toward souvenirs that satisfy one or more of the following criteria:

- inexpensive (or, better yet, FREE)
- part of an already established collection (preferably one that doesn't take up much space)
- consumable (no need to store it forever)
- wearable (and donate-able once it's outgrown)
- useful (something that serves a specific purpose)

This isn't to say we never buy souvenirs that don't fall into any of these categories. We do. My husband is especially fond of buying family-heirloom-type pieces during our travels—bronze or porcelain statues, marble book ends, world globes—but I do my best to persuade him not to purchase anything without first deciding exactly where it will go when we get back home.

-87-
Consumable Souvenirs

L ike most people, our family has limited space at home. And if we aren't careful, we'll find ourselves inundated with clutter.

That's why I favor useful souvenirs that have a limited shelf life, whether I'm buying them for myself or for friends back at home.

- food products from the area you're visiting: fruit, nuts, chocolate, candies, honey, jams, etc. (be sure to check travel restrictions if you plan to transport food items across state lines or national borders)
- art supplies: coloring books, craft kits, watercolors, chalk, colored pencils, etc.
- personal care products: hand crafted soap, lotion, perfume, bath salts, etc.
- paper products: stationery, postcards, notepads, etc.
- memberships: annual admission to affiliated zoos or museums

Incidentally, these are the same categories we suggest for Christmas gifts to/from extended family. ☺

-88-
Badges, Patches and Stickers

Yes, I realize stickers seldom serve a practical purpose other than being cute or funny, but they're also nice and flat and don't take up much room.

Besides, a couple of our kids love them—mainly our teen daughters, who like to stick them on their laptop covers and Nalgene bottles. Stickers also fit nicely into scrapbooks, adding interest to pages dedicated to photos from our trips.

The same thing can be said of the badges and patches our kids have earned through the Junior Ranger Program, too. (see Chapter 55) Those fit three of the criteria listed on the preceding page: they're small, collectable, *and* free. The only thing they cost is the little bit of time it takes to complete the learning activities required to earn them.

Most National Parks have custom ink stamps you can use for free when you visit, as well. You can even buy a "passport" in the park gift shop (or make your own at home) and use it to collect stamps from all the parks you visit.

117

-89-
Silver Charms

I once had a good friend who had a silver chain bracelet that was simply loaded with charms. She must have had two or three charms hanging from every link. It was truly a one-of-a-kind piece of jewelry.

And do you know where most of her charms came from? Her travels! She could go through every single charm, rattling off where it came from and what she was doing when she got it.

Instead of bringing home some kitschy figurine or other trinket that would collect dust on a bookshelf, she spent a dollar or two on a pretty little charm every time she took a trip, then attached it to a beautiful bracelet she wore all the time to serve as a reminder of all the good times she's had.

I love this concept and thought about copying it, but quickly gave up on the idea because (1) my wrist is too big for standard silver charm bracelets to fit comfortably and (2) the charms kept getting hooked in my hair and pulling loose. Which is really why I'm not much a jewelry person to begin with. But if you do like wearing jewelry, you'll want to keep this possibility in mind. It's definitely a keeper!

-90-
Pressed Pennies

Pressed penny machines may go the way of the dodo bird if the US Mint ever stops coining copper cents. But every bill Congress has put forward calling for the cessation of penny production has thus far failed. This, despite the fact pennies lose us money—it purportedly costs the government 1.5 times the face value of a penny to produce a penny.

So, for the time being, those little make-your-own-souvenir-pressed-penny booths are safe. Which is why you'll still find them at lots of popular tourist spots. For the cost of a couple of quarters, you can flatten a penny (which you must provide yourself) into an oblong disk embossed with the name and logo of the whatever attraction you're visiting.

Need help organizing your collection? Buy a pressed penny passport book (similar to the ones designed for collecting National Park stamps). Or punch a hole in the pennies and store them on a key ring or a charm bracelet.

-91-
Christmas Ornaments

The nice thing about buying Christmas ornaments as souvenirs is that every year while decorating your tree, you'll be reminded of all the exciting tips you've taken and all the wonderful vacation memories you've stored up.

Here again, you know exactly where the memento will go before you ever bring it home. In this case, you only take it out to look at for a short time every December. Then it gets put away for eleven more months, and you don't have to dust or clean it the rest of the year.

Sometimes, I press our kids' vacation keepsakes into service as Christmas décor, too—things they aren't ready to part with but serve no practical purpose, either, except to clutter up our living space. That's why, if you visit our house at Christmas time, you'll find Mardi Gras beads from New Orleans, sea shells from Hilton Head, and colored rock key chains from the Grand Canyon hanging on our tree next to the more traditional *bona fide* ornaments.

-92-
Stones & Shells

Every time we go the the beach, our children find a mound of treasures they want to bring home with them: shells, snails, seaweed, smooth stones, small pebbles, pieces of sea glass and coral, bivalves, sometimes even a crab or two.

But Dad usually limits them to keeping only two or three pieces—*and nothing sticky, stinky, or still alive*! Everything else gets tossed back into the ocean.

Even so, with enough trips to the beach over enough summers with enough children in tow, even our three-at-a-time quota adds up to quite the collection.

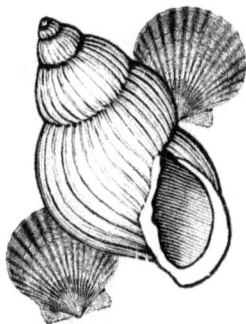

Do your children bring home more beach finds than you know what to do with? If they don't mind mixing their treasures together, try displaying them in a large, lidded jar.

Or do as I alluded to in Chapter 90: Add a string to hang the prettier ones on your Christmas tree. Or glue them on a picture frame and use it to display one of your vacation photos—taken at the beach, of course!

-93-
Coins, Stamps,
& Postcards

For our children who love collecting coins, a handful of foreign change is one of the best souvenirs they can imagine—and it saves us stopping by the currency exchange desk on our way back home. We just divvy up the little bit we have left between the numismatists in the family.

Postcards are also plentiful, practical, and inexpensive. Many visitor centers even offer a limited selection of free postcards. We seldom turn these down, as they make nice mementos, whether you use them to mail messages to family members or friends or save them to glue in your own scrapbook or collector's album.

If you choose to send your postcards home by mail, you'll need to locate a post office, as well. That will also give any philatelists in your family an opportunity to add to their stamp collections, as well.

-94-
Browse the Local Walmart

Before heading to a high-priced souvenir shop, consider visiting the local Walmart instead. Often stores in popular tourist towns offer a wide variety of related merchandise at a fraction of what you'd pay elsewhere.

When my husband and I finally did take our kids to Orlando a few years back, we followed our own advice and went shopping at a Walmart not far from the Magic Kingdom.

There I scored an adorable pair of fur-lined, glittery blue *Frozen* house slippers for my youngest daughter. I found them on a clearance rack for only $4. Other good grocery store finds were bubble wands, glow-in-the-dark necklaces, and fleece bathrobes (also on clearance) that our boys wrapped up in after swimming in the hotel pool and wore for several winters at home before finally outgrowing them.

If you're an avid thrifter, you can even stock up on fitting "souvenirs" before you ever leave home, then mete them out once you reach your vacation destination. I've seen princess dresses, mouse ears, light sabers, character puzzles, and all sorts of other Disney paraphernalia at garage sales priced a fraction of what they cost new.

Section 12

Expect the
Unexpected

-95-
Stick Together

The best defense is a good offense, as they say. And this is certainly true of traveling with children. You've got to anticipate the fact your little ones may get distracted or wander off—especially if they are anything like most of our kids were growing up—and take proactive steps to ensure nobody gets lost or left behind. Here are a few of the tips we've used over the years to help everyone stick together:

- BUDDY UP—Assign every person in the family a partner. In our family, Mom is usually paired with the youngest (especially when the youngest is a nursing baby), Dad gets the middle child, and each of the older kids is matched with a younger sibling.
- COUNT HEADS FREQUENTLY—Make sure every person in your party is present and accounted for. This should be done as a matter of routine, especially *every time* you load up in a car, bus, ship, train, or plane to travel from one place to another.
- WEAR MATCHING COLORS—It makes it easier to spot everybody (or for strangers to recognize the fact a stray child belongs to your group).

Technology can also help keep tabs on people in your party. Use cell phones or other tracking devices to reconnect if you get separated for awhile (intentionally or accidentally).

-96-
Lost & Found

Sometimes we can get split up, despite our best efforts to avoid it. We've taught our kids to follow a simple protocol anytime this happens:

Whoever's with Dad goes to search & everybody else stays put

We first instituted this rule before a three-week backpacking trip to Europe. Knowing how many planes, trains, buses and boats we'd likely board/disembark during our time abroad, we figured we'd better have a rule in place in the event we ever got separated.

Good thing we discussed it beforehand! We needed it when the doors of a Frankfurt tram snapped shut with Mom, Dad, and two babies still inside, then sped away while all our other seven children stood on a street corner and watched in dismay. Our oldest son kept his siblings in line until Dad and company found our way back to them. Thereafter, we made sure one parent always went first whenever we got on or off any mode of transportation while the other brought up the rear. That way, if we were ever separated again, Mom would be there to watch over the ones charged with waiting while Dad headed up the search party.

-97-
Tie-Dyed T-Shirts

I've already divulged the fact our family usually dresses in coordinating colors when we travel. I also mentioned that we sometimes buy T-shirts on vacation.

Well, some of the best investments we've ever made in the category of "wearable souvenirs" were some matching tie-dyed T-shirts for everyone in the family. We got one set of blue tie-dyes in Jamaica (with the words "Smile, Mon" embroidered across the front) and another set in rainbow shades from New Orleans.

Those shirts are our go-to uniforms anytime we anticipate being in a large crowd. They stand out like a sore thumb and allow us to instantly recognize where all our children are at a single glance. We've worn them at State Fairs, to Disney World, in foreign countries, to sporting events—anytime there's a higher-than-normal risk of losing somebody in a crowd. The only time this strategy failed us was when we inadvertently visited Six Flags (dressed in our rainbow tie-dyed tees) on Gay Pride Day. The park was packed, but on *that visit*, we blended in like camo in a rainforest!

129

-98-
Survival Supplies

An important principle we've tried to drive home with our children is the idea of anticipating unintended consequences:

- If you bat the ball toward the house, you may break a window.
- If you leave your laptop laying on the floor, somebody might step on it.
- If you skip studying for your final exam, you may fail the test.

In the same way, before heading out on a long road trip, you need think through potential problems and make allowances for them:

- Driving through the desert? Fill your gas tank, empty your bladder, and pack some extra water (for the people riding and the radiator) before setting out.
- Heading to the beach? Pack sunscreen, towels, sun glasses, and something to brush the sand off before getting back in the car.
- Hiking through the jungle? Wear insect repellent and comfortable shoes.
- Driving through snow-covered mountains? Bring tire chains, blankets, and a bag of cat litter (for traction).

-99-
Throw Up Buckets

If you'll be driving through many mountain passes with lots of children in the car, I'd recommend bringing along a couple of dishpans, too. Especially if any of said children are prone to motion sickness.

This is one tip we developed the hard way. After driving to dizzying heights on a trip to Northern California to admire the Giant Sequoias, our family unwittingly stopped a mile short of seeing the General Sherman Tree with its 36½ ft. diameter.

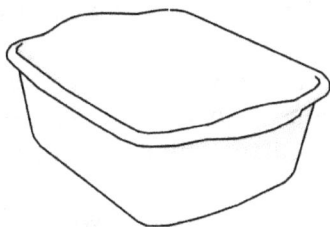

That's because, during our winding trip up the mountain, we became distracted by grazing deer, melting snowdrifts, a glorious sunset...and the vomiting child in our backseat! One of our little guys got queasy on the ascent, and a dishpan would have come in very handy for keeping things contained when he started throwing up!

So be sure to stash a couple of these "throw up buckets" under the seat anytime you expect a drive to be particularly tortuous. A prophylactic dose of Dramamine wouldn't hurt, either, for any passengers who need it.

-100-
Wet Wipes, Trash Bags, and Paper Towels

In addition to storing a couple of dishpans under your car seat for those susceptible to motion sickness, you might want to bring along extra supplies to make clean ups easy.

Paper towels, trash bags, and a canister of disinfecting wipes prove immensely practical when traveling—whether you have sick passengers or not.

Paper towels help with spills. Clorox wipes deal with sticky or contaminated surfaces. And trash bags allow you to easily gather up the rubbish.

And, believe me, taking a 3000-mile road trip with a dozen people in the van generates a fair share of rubbish! So we keep an ample supply of recycled grocery bags in a small canister in the door of our van.

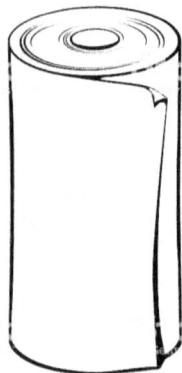

We pull one of them out every time we stop and clear all the trash out of the van: empty bottles, paper napkins, empty wrappers, stray straws, etc. That keeps the car tidy and the parents happy! ☺

-101-
First Aid Kit

A well-stocked first-aid kit is one essential no car should be without. As noted in Chapter 30, we keep a small stash of our most-commonly needed supplies (Band-Aids, ear drops, antacid, ibuprofen) in the toiletry bag we carry into the hotel with us. But we stow a more thorough set of medical supplies in a zipper pouch in the car. It includes all of the following:

- bandages in multiple sizes
- a small tube of anti-biotic ointment
- sugar tablets (for our kids with Type 1 diabetes)
- Tylenol/ Advil (child and adult formulas)
- Triaminic Cough & Cold strips
- travel sized bottle of Tums
- a sample of diaper rash ointment
- travel-sized hand sanitizer
- small tube of Orajel
- gauze
- scissors
- medical tape
- alcohol wipes
- eye drops
- ear drops
- Dramamine

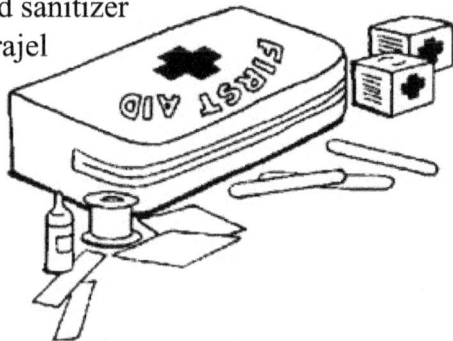

Traveling
with Baby

-102-
Pack a Port-a-Crib

Back when we had a whole vanful of little ones, we invested in a couple of pack-n-play cribs and took them with us every time we traveled.

They were fast and easy to put up and take down. Compact and lightweight, they didn't take up much luggage space and normally fit nicely in the space between the dresser and the door (on the opposite side of the room from the air conditioner, so babies didn't get chilled at night).

Hotels will often provide a fold-up crib if you don't already have one, but I prefer the consistency of putting babies to bed in the same one every night.

Still, even our own port-a-cribs seemed strange and new to our little ones the first time we took them on a road trip. If I had any doubt as to whether a baby would go to bed easily in the unfamiliar crib, I'd set it up at home a week before we planned to leave, so baby could get used to sleeping in it beforehand.

I also made custom, padded sheets for both our cribs out of preschooler-pleasing prints (*Spiderman!*), which went a long way toward making our babies happy to go to sleep in a new place. A few of them even begged to be put to bed early.

-103-
Crank Up the Music

S ome of our babies traveled better than others. For those who had trouble, we tried every trick in the book to keep them happy on the road.

We'd talk to them, sing songs, read books, shake toys, and do our best to keep them entertained. If that didn't work, we'd get really quiet, not make eye contact, and pretend to sleep ourselves.

Probably the most impressive response we got for all our efforts came from a 12-month-old Rebekah on a 3000-mile road trip. She didn't travel very well on that trip, due to a lingering ear infection and emerging molars.

So it's a good thing we had John Denver in the glove box. She didn't care for any other song on the CD, but would immediately stop crying, cock her head to one side, and grin from ear to ear every time we played (and replayed and replayed and replayed) "Thank God I'm a Country Boy!"

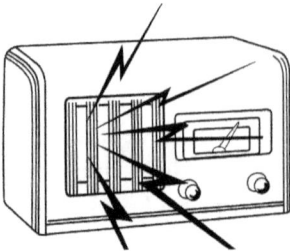

We listened to that song for hours on end. Even today, whenever I hear it, I'm immediately transported back in time to that foot-stomping, hand-clapping, yee-hawing road trip!

-104-
The Unassuming Umbrella Stroller

When I was pregnant with our first baby, I received an invitation in the mail to attend a special, free seminar for expectant parents—complete with door prizes! Being the bargain hunter I was, I immediately signed up to attend. It was really just an elaborate marketing gimmick. We were cajoled into thinking all our future parenting problems could be solved by buying a Wonder Chair. The chrome-and-vinyl fringed edition would convert from a pram to a bassinet to a stroller to a high chair to a rocker. And all for *only $700!*

The pitch was convincing—*how would we ever raise a baby without one?*—but we couldn't afford the price tag. Which was a blessing, since I later spotted that same deluxe model at a garage sale for $15 (and eventually sold it for $20 at my own after realizing what a hassle it was to use the thing)!

We've had a variety of strollers over the years, but umbrella strollers are still our all-time favorite. They're lightweight, compact, inexpensive, and easy to pop up and take down. We still have one, even though it's been years since our kids were small enough to ride in one. Now we use it solely for toting snacks and drinks around theme parks that let guests carry food in (including Legoland and most Disney parks).

-105-
Nursing on the Road

If you've ever dealt with a colicky baby, you know how inconsolable they can be. We had one daughter who screamed five hours solid every evening—from 7:00 to midnight. And she'd cry even louder whenever we buckled her into a car seat.

We did very little traveling when that child was an infant. But occasionally we would brave a weekend trip to visit grandparents. Unfortunately, they lived eight hours away.

That's a long time to listen to an unhappy baby! If you have a little one who doesn't travel well, postpone as many trips as you can until the baby's a little older. Otherwise, try the following suggestions:

- travel at times the baby normally sleeps
- sing to baby or play soothing music (see Chapter 103)
- pull over to nurse/ burp the baby
- pump your milk in advance and feed with bottle

We tried all this and more for our baby girl. The only way I could keep her quiet for long, though, was by hunching over her car seat and nursing on the road (so we could both stay strapped in). It was admittedly very uncomfortable, but it sure beat listening to her cry for eight hours straight!

-106-
A Well-Stocked Diaper Bag

Babies are predictably unpredictable. They spit up. They have massive blow outs. They throw pacifiers and shoes and hair bows out the window when you aren't looking. So it's important to come prepared whenever a baby's onboard.

That being said, we've found that the vast majority of what our generation considered "essential" for baby care was really just extra weight. We usually carried a small diaper bag stocked with only the most basic items:

- dipes and wipes
- extra change of clothes
- pacifier
- nursing blanket
- snack (cheerios or goldfish)
- formula & bottles (for the baby I had to supplement)
- maybe a toy (though the best entertainment is MOM)

Many times, we'd pare the essentials down even further, leaving our bag in the car (for emergencies) and toting only a single diaper and a Ziploc of wipes in our back pocket.

-107-
Put the Pacie on a Leash

There's nothing like making it out to the middle of nowhere, only to discover your baby's pacifier was accidentally lost or left behind at your last stop (refer to Chapter 85).

Experience speaking: It takes a long time to drive across the great state of Texas, but if feels a hundred times longer when you're riding in the car with a screaming baby!

Do yourself a favor. Tether the pacifier and clip it to the baby's onesie. That way, when he pulls the plug out of his mouth and drops it by the wayside, you can reel it right back in the minute you need it.

Leashes work well for favorite toys, too. I wish we'd put one on our oldest son's "diabetic dog" when he took it along with us to the Dallas Zoo back when he was four.

That would have saved us (and the zookeepers) a huge hassle when our boy dropped it into an animal enclosure during the monorail ride. It took over an hour for park personnel to find and retrieve it.

Section 14

International Travel

-108-
Passport Photos

You'll need a passport for every member of your family if you plan on traveling internationally. Those for kids under 18 are only good for five years, so even if you already have passports, check to make sure they're all still valid.

Pro tip for saving money on passports: apply early (to avoid expediting fees) and take your own photos. Sure, you can get passport photos fast at local drugstores or in the passport office, but they'll charge you up to $10 a pop per pic. If you're already paying for a dozen or more passports, why not line the family up at home, print out a few 2x2s, and save yourself a cool hundred or more? Just follow these easy guidelines:

- stand in front of a solid white background
- no hats, sunglasses, or uniforms of any kind
- make sure there are no shadows on or around you
- face forward and keep your eyes WIDE OPEN

Otherwise, they'll reject your photos and your efforts will be wasted. You can also follow this link to download an easy-to-use template: *http://bit.ly/passportphototemplate*

-109-
Learn the Language

Although there is no shortage of English speakers in most industrialized countries, it is always a good idea to learn at least a few basic phrases in the native tongue of your host country whenever you're traveling abroad.

At a minimum, I'd recommend knowing how to say *hello, goodbye, please, thank you,* and *you're welcome,* as well as how to ask general directions, locate a bathroom, order food, and exchange money.

If you carry a smart phone, Google Translate can help you out, assuming you can get good reception in the area you are visiting. Otherwise, I'd recommend taking a few online classes or investing in a program like Pimsleur.

Pimsleur offers 30-lesson courses in virtually every language most vacationers will ever need. Our entire family studied German, French, and Italian this way before backpacking Europe for the first time.

That was in the era before smart phones, but we learned enough of all three languages that we were able to carry on basic conversations in all the countries we visited—even with the non-English speaking owners of a guesthouse we stayed in for the three days we were in Austria.

-110-
Study Culture Beforehand

Language will only get you so far in a foreign country. It is important to also learn something about their culture and customs, if you can. Body language speaks volumes, and you do not want to offend anybody by sending rude signals unawares.

- Some gestures that are considered friendly in one country (including the signs for *victory*, *peace*, and *okay*) are considered vulgar in another, so avoid using hand signals unless you know for sure
- In India and Japan, proper etiquette requires you to finish all the food on your plate. But in China, you should leave a bite or two untouched. Your host will feel insulted if you clean your plate.
- It's bad manners to burp after a meal in some countries, but the Chinese consider it a compliment.
- If you are given anything in Japan—a gift, a business card, a stack of towels by the hotel staff—you should accept it with both hands. To do otherwise is seen as rude and ungrateful.

147

-111-
Air Travel Tips

Taking young children on a plane ride for any amount of time is a special challenge, but if you are planning a trans-Atlantic flight, you'll want to be doubly prepared:

- pack chewing gum or lollipops to help normalize the pressure in your kids' ears while in flight
- bring magnetic games or activity books to keep them entertained
- use triangular shaped crayons or colored pencils to keep them from rolling off the tray table
- pack a favorite pillow, blanket, or lovey to help them sleep on long flights
- stash some light snacks in your carry-on bag in case they get hungry
- sit close enough to the bathrooms to get there quickly, but not so close the noise keeps them awake

-112-
Cruising with Children

We took our first cruise in 2002. The bottom had dropped out of the travel industry as a result of 9/11, so we got an incredible deal when we booked our passage.

We had a blast cruising with our kids. Here's a short list of essentials you'll be glad you packed when you take your children cruising:

SEASICKNESS REMEDIES: Tuck some Dramamine or a couple of Scopolamine patches into your suitcase to deal with any queasiness you feel while onboard the ship. My only regret is that I took off my patch as soon as I disembarked at the end of our trip. The room kept rocking for two more days, and I wish I'd had the Scopolamine in my system a little longer to deal with that.

SUN PROTECTION: Don't let sunburned skin spoil your vacation. Pack plenty of sunblock and slather up before hitting the beach. A good pair of sunglasses and a wide-brimmed hat are helpful, too.

JACKET OR HOODIE: The deck can get a little chilly, especially after dark. Take along a light jacket to stay warm. You'll be glad you have one if you decide to watch any of the poolside movies shown after sunset.

SOMETHING TO READ: Relaxing on the beach or beside the pool is more enjoyable when you have a good book with you. (It also provides a nice diversion when you're cooped up in the cabin with napping babies.)

PEN AND PAPER: Our cell phones didn't work while we were on the ship, but a few sticky notes and a ballpoint pen allowed us to keep everybody in our group abreast of each other's whereabouts. I'd post the day's schedule on our door each morning, so our older children would know where to find us on the ship at any given time.

DRESS CLOTHES: Tanks and flip-flops aren't usually allowed in the formal dining room, so we brought along a sport coat for each of our boys and nice dresses for the girls. The little ones really seemed to enjoy getting spiffed up for dinner.

CASH: Instead of booking shore excursions through the cruise line in advance, we saved a bundle by negotiating prices ourselves once we reached the port. Carrying cash made it all that much easier to do so.

WET WIPES: The showers in the cabin were cramped, and our kids spent most of the day in the pool anyway, so we usually made due with cleaning their hands and feet with a wet wipe before bed and calling it good. They're handy for wiping up spills and other unexpected messes, too.

CAMERA: There are lots of great memories to be made on any family vacation, and a cruise is no exception. Be sure you bring a camera along to capture a few for the photo albums.

LANYARDS: Help your kids keep up with their room keys: hang them around their necks. Lanyards are available on the ship, but cost ten times what you'd pay back home. So stop by the Dollar Store on your way to the port and buy one for everybody in your party.

*Solution to the brain teaser in Chapter 44:

Point to either of the two paths and phrase your question like this: "If I were to ask you if this is the path to the port, would you say YES?"

If it is the right path, and you're speaking to a truth teller, he'll answer YES (because he will indeed say YES if you ask him whether the right path is the right path).

If it is the right path, and you're speaking to a perpetual liar, he'll lie and claim that he'd say YES (because he will actually answer in the negative if you ask him whether the right path is the right path).

If it's the wrong path, and you're speaking to a truth teller, he'll say NO (because he would never answer affirmatively if you asked him whether the wrong path is the right path).

If it's the wrong path, and you're speaking to a perpetual liar, he'll lie and claim that he'd answer NO (because he'd really say yes if you ask him whether the wrong path is the right path).

Either way, by phrasing your one question in this manner, you'll get the correct answer, regardless which tribe the native you're addressing hails from.

- AFTERWORD -

Well, that brings us to the end of the book! I hope what you've read has motivated you to think outside the box when it comes to planning family vacations, and that you've also learned some good tips for saving money as you travel.

As nice as it is to occasionally "get away" for an extended holiday, the real secret for making wonderful memories with your children is to connect with them on a daily basis. Don't try to pack all the fun into two weeks a year—instead, take frequent breaks at home to talk and share and explore and learn and play games together.

No summer trip to Disney can compete with the magic of living in a home with a family who loves one another and delights in spending time together, all year long.

So take what you've gleaned from *Pack Up & Leave* and give the ideas that resonate with your family's goals, personalities, and particular circumstances a try. Then let me know how it goes.

May God bless and protect you as you go,

Jennifer Flanders

www.flandersfamily.info
www.facebook.com/TheFlandersFamily

more titles in this series:

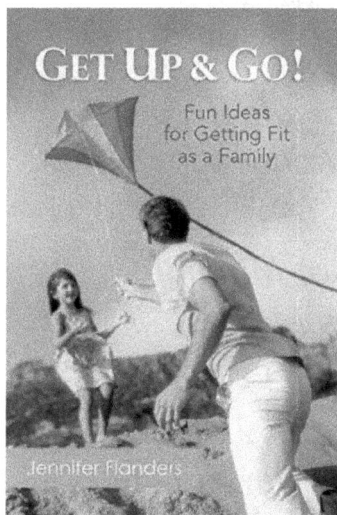

GET UP & GO: Do you have a hard time fitting a workout into your already busy schedule? Are all the individual sports practices and fitness routines eating into family time or sending you in different directions every night of the week? If you are looking for fresh ideas for getting your children up and moving in a way that doesn't fragment your family, look no further. All you need is a little GET UP & GO!

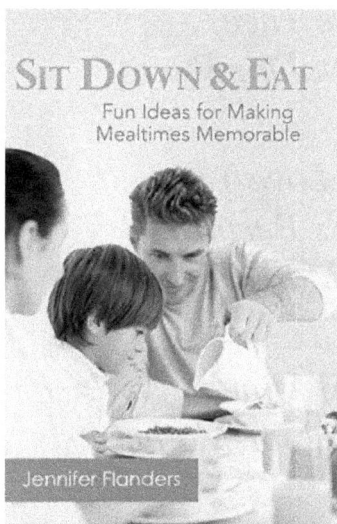

SIT DOWN & EAT: If you can't remember the last time your family gathered around a dinner table for a leisurely, home-cooked meal with every member present and engaged in a single conversation (no cell phones or surreptitious texting allowed!), then this is the book for you. In it, you'll find a wealth of ideas for reclaiming the family dinner hour for use in building up your loved ones and creating positive memories together.

- MORE BOOKS -
by Jennifer Flanders

*25 Ways to Communicate Respect
to Your Husband: A Handbook for Wives*

*Balance: The Art of Minding
What Matters Most*

*Glad Tidings: The First 25 Years
of Flanders Family Christmas Letters*

*How Do I Love Thee?
A Devotional Journal for Wives*

*Love Your Husband/ Love Yourself:
Embracing God's Purpose
for Passion in Marriage*

*Sweet Child of Mine:
A Devotional Journal for Mothers*

- OTHER TITLES -
from Prescott Publishing

25 Ways to Show Love to Your Wife:
A Handbook for Husbands
by Doug Flanders, MD

How to Encourage Your Husband:
Ideas to Revitalize Your Marriage
by Nancy Campbell

How to Encourage Your Children:
Tools to Help You Raise Mighty Warriors for God
by Nancy Campbell

Life's Big Questions
Colossians
by Doug Flanders, MD

The Sweet Gospel:
13 Weeks of Savoring the Good News
by Mandy Ballard

www.ingramcontent.com/pod-product-compliance
Lightning Source LLC
Chambersburg PA
CBHW071534040426
42452CB00008B/1009